A SHORT HISTORY OF THE PICTS

BY JÜRGEN DIETHE

ISBN: 978-1-905787-54-8

Printed by
For The Right Reasons
60 Grant Street, Inverness, IV3 8BS
fortherightreasons@rocketmail.com
Tel: 01463 718844

TABLE OF CONTENTS

INTRODUCTION

Writing a history of the Picts could make a very short volume if we were to restrict ourselves to what is known and what is certain. Gaps are inevitable, and so is a degree of speculation. Of course, we have come a very long way in terms of academic research from the days when even the Picts' origin and their language were a matter of more or less informed guesswork at best, when beyond a skeleton of facts – or rather: possible facts – provided by the Venerable Bede, the Irish chronicles and the somewhat dubious "*Pictish Chronicle*" we had very little to go by. And the carved stones, of course, but their strange symbolism served, if anything, to deepen the mystery. The character and volume of written sources has not changed, but some gaps have been filled by background information provided by archaeology (which has a long way to go yet), and historians have simply become much better at using all the tools at their service to make the inevitable speculation more informed and to consign more and more myths to where they belong, in the dustbin of history. And this includes, as we shall see, the violent takeover of the Pictish state by Kenneth McAlpin's Scots. Even so, informed readers of this small book will perhaps find reason to disagree with some or much which they will read here. The many qualifications, in terms of "perhaps", "may", "possibly" etc. indicate the flimsiness of the foundation on which many new interpretations stand, which I have drawn from the latest academic literature on the subject. But the old interpretations had equally flimsy or, rather, even weaker foundations.

In some ways it seems as though the Picts arose from the mists of early Scottish history and disappeared again in an equally mysterious fashion, leaving just highly impressive witnesses hewn out of stone. When BBC radio ran a series on "the lost peoples of Europe" and included the Picts, it served to underline this impression. They seemed to be wholly separate from the Scotland of today that boasts largely Gaelic origins. The Picts have been characterised in numerous ways, first by the Romans as a people with body paint or tattoos. They had undoubtedly a ferocious reputation, they were rumoured to be small, with long arms, as some mythical sources alleged, living in underground houses – the souterrains were at one point called "Pictish houses", and the Brochs "Pictish towers" (we now know that all these were pre-Pictish, and the souterrains were most likely used for storage). In short, they were the subject of endless myths and misinformation, and Bede did not help by placing their origin in Scythia.

There is no need to rehash all these old stories. This small book tries to give the Picts their real place in the course of Scottish or, if one so wishes, pre-Scottish history and show the way in which the Picts are very much present, even today. It is based not on my own research (I am no medievalist) but on the latest state of academic literature on the Picts and the history of the "dark ages" in Scotland and the neighbouring territories with which they interacted, mainly Gaelic Dalriada, Germanic (Anglian) Northumbria and the Britons of Strathclyde – and finally, of course, the Vikings, who decisively changed the relationship between Picts and Scots, albeit not immediately. They were the "joker" in this dark age power-play.

Living, as I do, on the Black Isle, I could hardly fail to notice the Picts, with the Groam House Museum in Rosemarkie and its splendid Pictish cross slab, with the equally impressive cross slab in Nigg church, with Portmahomack, with Sueno's Stone in Forres and Pictish sites like Craig Phadraig, Knockfarrell, Burghead and others in the vicinity. I feel that not enough is made of these momentous remains, compared with the rather weaker Gaelic presence in this region. I am also very lucky to know Elizabeth Sutherland, who used to live in our present house in Fortrose and who has become a good friend. She is one of the leading authorities on the Picts, and I have had many fruitful conversations with her.

A short word about names: I have generally used the most familiar versions, which are often anglicised, as in Kenneth McAlpin, Constantine or Donald etc., in order to improve readability. Sometimes I add alternative, more accurate versions in terms of their historical use. This varied anyway, depending on the language used by the sources, which could alternate between Latin, Gaelic or Pictish.

ORIGINS

It is well known that the name "Picts" has Roman origins, first used in the year 297 AD, in a poem by a certain Eumenius in praise of the emperor Constantius Chlorus. It simply means "the painted people", although when the fifth-century poet Claudian in a poem on the defeat of a rebellion in Italy through General Stilicho mentions the Picts in connection with a legion left behind in Britain, he speaks of strange shapes tattooed on the faces of dying Picts – tattoo being a translation of "marking with iron" ("ferro picta, ferroque notates"). It is unlikely that there was anything like a Pictish identity in the late Roman period, and we know that the indigenous Britons called them "Priteni", i.e. Britons. It is an interesting speculation that the names Britons and Britain might have their origin in an external appellation of the Picts. Incidentally, we have no idea how they described themselves, because this is the most vexing aspect of Pictish history: we have no written material by the Picts themselves, apart from a very few carved inscriptions in Latin that only serve to identify individuals.

So what about their origin? The Venerable Bede, an Anglian monk who lived from 673 to 735 and spent most of his adult life in the Bernician monastery of Jarrow where he wrote his main work, *The Ecclesiastical History of the English People* (English people being "gens Anglorum" in the Latin original), is responsible for a lot of the confusion. This was how he characterised the British Isles, after a description of the land itself:

At the present time, there are five languages in Britain
…. These are the English, British, Irish, Pictish, as well
as the Latin languages; through the study of the scrip-
tures, Latin is in general use among them all. To begin
with, the inhabitants of the island were all Britons, from
whom it receives its name; they sailed to Britain, so it is
said, from the land of Armorica [in Gaul], and appro-
priated to themselves the southern part of it. After they
had got possession of the greater part of the island, beginning from the south, it is related that the Pictish race
from Scythia sailed out into the ocean in a few warships
and were carried by the wind beyond the furthest
bounds of Britain, reaching Ireland and landing on its
northern shores. There they found the Irish race and
asked permission to settle among them but their request was refused. Now Ireland is the largest island of
all next to Britain, and lies to the west of it. … The
Picts then came to this island, as we have said, by sea
and asked for the grant of a place to settle in. The Irish
answered that the island would not hold them both;
'but', said they, 'we can give you some good advice as to
what to do. We know of another island not far from
our own, in an easterly direction, which we often see in
the distance on clear days. If you will go there, you can
make a settlement for yourselves; but if any one resists
you, make use of our help.' And so the Picts went to
Britain and proceeded to occupy the northern parts of
the island, because the Britons had seized the southern
regions. As the Picts had no wives, they asked the Irish

for some; the latter consented to give them women, only on condition that, in all cases of doubt, they should elect their kings from the female royal line rather than the male; and it is well known that the custom has been observed among the Picts to this day. In the course of time Britain received a third tribe in addition to the Britons and the Picts, namely the Irish. These came from Ireland under their leader Reuda, and won lands among the Picts either by friendly treaty or by the sword. These they still possess. They are still called Dalreudini after this leader, *Dal* in their language signifying a part.

Here Bede speaks of Dalriada, the West Scottish region that more or less corresponds with the modern Argyll and had been settled by Gaelic-speaking Scots from Ireland – when these "Scotti" (this was the Roman name for the Irish) came to Scotland is entirely unclear.

When the origin of the Picts was indeed a matter of speculation, as was their language, Bede's version was taken seriously, to the degree that people believed that the Picts had settled in Britain separately from the Celtic-speaking Britons. Scythia was clearly impossible, being near the Caspian Sea from where ships could not be launched in the direction of Britain or anywhere. Perhaps he had meant Scandia, i.e. Scandinavia, and they had arrived from the North? Another Irish legend had them coming through Roman territory from Thracia, they had settled in Ireland until they had become too powerful and were driven away, but not until they had taken Irish wives. There is another legend concerning the origin of the Picts, which was a later construction from the High Middle Ages when the Picts as an entity had long disappeared. It is probably of Gaelic origin. According to this, the first Pictish king was called Cruithne, which was the Gaelic version of "Priteni". He had reigned for a hundred years, and after his death his seven sons divided the kingdom amongst themselves and reigned for another 250 years. The names of the sons and the districts they ruled were given as Fib, Fidach, Fotlaig, Fortrenn, Cait, Ce and Circinn. This is found in a Gaelic poem in the medieval Irish history *Lebor Gabála*, probably from the second half of the ninth century:

> Morsheimer do Cruithne clainn
> Raindset Albain i secht raind;
> Cait, Cé, Cirig, cétach clan
> Fib, Fidach, Fotla, Fortrenn
> Ocus is o ainm gach fir dib fil for a fearand.

> Seven sons of Cruithen
> Divided Alba into seven parts,
> Cait, Cé, Cirig, a warlike clan,
> Fife, Fidach, Fotla and Fortrenn
> And each name remains in his own country.

This is clearly a literary translation of real territories – Fid being Fife, Fotlaig Atholl, Cait describes Caithness, Circinn is connected in medieval sources with Angus and The Mearns, and Fortrenn was usually called Fortriu, which was traditionally located in the fertile area round Perth, although recent research has placed it on the southern coast of the Moray Firth. However, Fidach has also been connected with the counties of Ross and Moray. Cirig and Fotla have not been identified success-fully.

But what about the real origins? The Romans have been less than helpful there. While today's England was a largely peaceful province, less troublesome than many others, they never got to grips with Scotland. The most serious attempt to conquer Scotland was undertaken in 83 AD under the emperor Domitian with an army led by Agricola. We are reasonably well informed about this through Agricola's biography penned by his son-in-law, Tacitus. If we can believe what he writes, the campaign was a great success, a Roman fleet sailed at least as far north as the Moray Firth, while Agricola's four legions, by this time somewhat weakened and probably not as strong as the 28,000 claimed by Tacitus, defeated a vast Caledonian army of 30,000 men with war chariots (an equally unlikely number), led by a warrior called Calgacus, at a place called "Mons Graupius". Perhaps it should have been "Mons Grampius" and referred to the Grampian Mountains, which would at least place the battle into a likely territory. While a victory was claimed, it was never followed up, because domestic circumstances in Rome compelled Agricola to withdraw. The Romans will also have noticed that the wild and inhospitable Scotland with its harsh climate had very little to offer them, and they settled down behind Hadrian's Wall for centuries, only briefly holding a forward line around what is now Edinburgh and Glasgow, in the shape of the much less elaborate Antonine Wall. Whether Hadrian's Wall was first and foremost a military fortification or also served to control trade and the delivery of tribute payments, possibly even by the Romans to keep troublesome neighbours quiet, is not entirely clear. In 209 AD, the emperor Septimius Severus made the last attempt to conquer or effectively pacify Scotland, when he personally led an army north. He was successful, but when he died in York in 211, his son Caracalla gave up his father's campaign to secure for himself the emperorship in Rome. There were various military engagements in the course of the fourth century but no organised attempt to conquer Scotland – by this time, Rome was generally on the defensive.

Around 150 AD, the Alexandrian geographer Claudius Ptolemaeus (Ptolemy) made an attempt to name the various tribes that made up the northern British population, likely to be based on information provided earlier by Agricola. In this context, it is worth mentioning the Votadini who lived in southeast Scotland, in the Roman sphere of influence north of Hadrian's Wall. Their territory included today's Edinburgh and was called Gododdin, which can easily be identified as Celtic, close to today's Welsh. To the west of them lived the Britons of Strathclyde, a name used much later, who inhabited a surprisingly stable entity that at times stretched all the way down to and including the English Lake District. The most important Scottish tribe were the Caledonii, a name which the Romans continued to use, even referring occasionally to "Caledonians and other Picts", which indicates that the Romans perceived some kind of state entity including Picts as early as the third and fourth centuries. Early in the third century, Cassius Dio, a Roman consul and historian (who wrote in Greek), spoke of two tribes in Scotland, Caledonii and Maeatae, and we can assume that those two are meant when later sources talk about Dicalydones and

Verturiones. We can also assume that those two tribes made up the Picts and also described the two parts of Pictland, which were not always united. Whether there was an embryonic Pictish "national consciousness" in the Roman period, is impossible to know, but there is no doubt that the Romans were the early catalyst of the growth of Pictish unity, a state entity which, at its height, after all embraced virtually the whole of Scotland north of the river Forth, including the Western and Northern Isles.

As the grip of the Roman empire weakened in the second half of the fourth century, the number of Pictish raids in England increased, culminating in the so-called "Barbarian Conspiracy" of 367-9, eased by a mutiny on Hadrian's Wall. Picts, Scots, "Attacotti" (about whom we know nothing) and allegedly even Saxons and Franks attacked and overwhelmed the Roman defences in Britain. For the last time, the Romans were able to re-conquer lost territory and restore order, but when the Britons asked Rome for help again in 410, Honorius, the first West-Roman emperor, turned the request down – Rome itself was fighting for its existence, having been sacked and plundered by the Visigoths. Subsequently, Scotland remained initially unaffected by the chaos that afflicted England when weak British territories were occupied by Germanic tribes, Saxon, Angles, Jutes, who constituted their own unstable state entities. Much is unclear about the German invasions, regarding, for instance, the size of the armies and the question how and whether the indigenous Celtic population was integrated. Gildas the Wise wrote that the British tribes had hired Saxon mercenaries to help fight the Picts, and these mercenar-

13

ies had then taken over, but it is likely that there were already many Germans in Britain as soldiers in the Roman army, and they simply stayed, with others following. But this need not detain us in this context.

All this leaves a much clearer perspective on the language spoken by the Picts, which, as I mentioned, had been the subject of a great deal of speculation, even as late as the 1950s. We can assume that after the Celtic migration any earlier languages, spoken, for instance, by the people who built Skara Brae on Orkney, had disappeared. People in Britain will have spoken Celtic languages throughout. Celtic has, still today, two main branches, named after a sound shift: P-Celtic and Q-Celtic. Today, P-Celtic comprises Welsh and Breton and also, until it died out, Cornish. Q-Celtic is spoken in Ireland and Scotland. In Roman times, Q-Celtic was restricted to Ireland and then migrated to Argyll, i.e. Dalriada, whereas Britain spoke P-Celtic – and that included Scotland. There are numerous P-Celtic geographic names in Scotland which point to the time before Gaelic spread across the country. The idea that the Picts spoke Gaelic can therefore be discounted – one credible piece of evidence is in Adomnan's life of St. Columba, where he writes that the saint needed an interpreter to converse with the Pictish king, although we may assume that the two Celtic branches were closer to each other than Welsh and Gaelic are today. We should also not over-interpret Bede's description of Pictish and British as separate languages; there will have been dialects, and it is unlikely that he actually spoke British, as he lived in an Anglo-Saxon kingdom and wrote in Latin.

EARLY CHRONOLOGY

There is a historical document that masquerades as Pictish history: the *Pictish Chronicle*. However, any hope of finding a coherent narration about the Picts is soon dashed. It is merely a list of kings with some, it seems arbitrary titbits of information, a list moreover that begins in a clearly mythical past but gains some semblance of credibility as it moves into the sixth and seventh centuries. The lack of credibility is hardly surprising when we consider that the chronicle is based on manuscripts the earliest of which appears to go back to around 970, and there are several versions. William Skene, the pioneer of Pictish studies in the 19th century, identified seven versions, which, however, seem to be based on two originals. But what is original? They have only come to us in later copies, written in Latin, or rather: copies of copies. Errors by the scribes are therefore more than likely.

The list begins with the legendary Cruithne and his seven sons, as mentioned above, and then carries on through many kings and many centuries, several reigns lasting a hundred years, one even 150 years. It is pointless adding these up, it would take us back into early British history probably before the arrival of the Celts. The last king before we reach something like historical credibility is described thus:

> Drust filius Erp c. annis regnavit et c. bella peregit; ix decimo anno regni ejus Patricius episcopus sanctus ad Hiberniam pervenit insulam. (Drust the son of Erp ruled for 100 years and fought 100 battles; in the 19th

year of his rule Saint Patrick the Bishop arrived in the island of Ireland.)

Now this gives us a rough date: St. Patrick is said to have arrived in Ireland in 432, although it could have been anytime between 430 and 470. This Drust must have been quite important – he is only one of three kings that get a description going beyond origin and length of reign. We can assume that he held the crown for a long period (the mythical hundred years) and was a successful warrior (the equally mythical hundred battles). And if we take the reference to Patrick seriously, and there is no reason why not, we have reached a point where some kind of Pictish identity had been established. After all, the Romans had long gone, and they had been the ones who had "given" the Scottish tribes their Pictish name and a degree of unity. The Picts were much feared during the chaotic conditions after the Roman withdrawal, were launching raids deep into Britain – if we can believe Gildas, Picts and Scots had at one point occupied the whole of Northern Britain, right down to Hadrian's Wall, in other words: the whole of today's Scotland. The Picts were feared almost as much as later the Vikings, whose victims the Picts themselves became. It is likely to have been this Drust who led his troops south through the Lowlands of today, until defeated by the Britons in the "Battle of the Caledonian Forest" ("bellum in silva caledonis"), as described by the Welsh monk Nennius in the *Historia Brittonum* in the 9th century. Traditionally, this battle is associated with the legendary King Arthur, but who knows whether he, too, might have had a Scottish connection?

If the Picts briefly occupied the Lowlands, it was quite untypical. Pictland, or Pictavia, as it was called in the Latin-language chronicles, lay north of the Forth-Clyde line, concentrated on the two most fertile stretches of land: the area from Perth (which is a Pictish name – in Welsh it means something like copse, wood) all the way to Fife, and then further north the lands around the Moray Firth. Today's Stirling probably marked the southern boundary. The Grampian Mountains between those core areas meant that the unity of Pictland was by no means always guaranteed, that the country may have been more often split into two entities than not. Another huge obstacle was the mountain range of the central Highlands, Druim Alban, the spine of Britain, which even now has only few roads leading through it. But there is evidence that the Hebrides were Pictish, or at least loosely connected to the Pictish kingdom, and that Orkney was quite firmly within the Pictish sphere of influence and, to a certain degree, also the Shetland Isles. There was one obvious route connecting northern Pictland with Dalriada – the Great Glen, which was the way St. Columba chose when he went to see the Pictish king at Inverness. Pictland was often, and especially in its later phase, associated with the name of Fortriu, which was traditionally located in the fertile lands east of Perth. Recent research by Alex Woolf has relocated Fortriu to the Moray Firth, which necessitates some re-writing of Pictish history. I remain to be convinced by this, because in the later period there appear to be some clear associations between southern Pictavia and Fortriu, as will become clear later.

If Pictland was therefore the early medieval predecessor of Scotland, it was much smaller than today's territory. I have already mentioned that British entities occupied the land south of the river Forth, the Britons of Strathclyde in the west (the name appears much later) and the Votadini of Manau Gododdin in the east. The major new power in the southeast were the Angles of Northumbria, for a long time split into the two state entities of Bernicia and Deira but later united. They were to destroy Gododdin and become the Picts' immediate neighbours, one of the major influences on Pictish history. The other neighbours, in Argyll, were the Scots of Dalriada, whose origin is also rather obscure. Traditionally it was said that they had come from Ireland in around 500, but it is likely that they had been there much longer, probably occupying a largely empty stretch of land. There was a Dalriada in Northern Ireland as well, and thus we can assume that there remained a fairly close connection across the sea to Ireland. Travelling by sea was normal and much easier than across inhospitable lands.

We know more about the Scots in Argyll than about the Picts, partly because of the Irish chronicles and partly because of an invaluable document called *Senchus fer n'Alban*, probably from the second half of the seventh century. It can best be described as a military census, listing the numbers of warriors from the various families and clans, for the army and the navy. We can assume that Dalriada may have had a population of around 25,000, and the *Senchus* indicates that the territory was more rigorously militarised than virtually any other entity in early medieval Europe. This was, indeed, somewhat unusual, as armies in Celtic and Germanic lands in this period tended to consist of small "war-bands" formed out of relations and retainers of kings and nobles – wars will not necessarily have involved the peasant population, only and very frequently as victims. It explains why the Scots managed to hold their own for long periods against the much more numerous Picts and also against the Britons of Strathclyde. The Pictish population, if we take Pictavia in its largest configuration, would have been around 100,000, on the basis of the fact that the whole of Scotland, including the Lowlands, had a population of around one million at the time of the English Civil War. We also know much more about the social structure of the Scots, not least because it was similar to conditions in Ireland – clan-based with kings and high kings. This will have been similar in Pictland, but there were no high kings there – if there were several kings in Pictavia it meant that the country was split or that they were engaged in a power struggle.

However, the social structure of the Picts will have been largely similar to that of the Scots, with the likely exception that there will have been less requirement for the peasant population to bear arms. Early medieval kings were not fundamentally different from other nobles, which is a typical characteristic of a clan-based society. We can assume that society was more structured in the more densely populated core areas with their fertile lands, whereas the thinly settled uplands or the more remote areas in the north and west will have been under looser control of the local lords, possibly even remnants of earlier virtually independent peasant communities. There will have been a system of tributes and payments in kind (there was certainly no money in Pictland), but we know nothing about this. The power basis of kings will have lain in their own tribes or clans (for instance the Verturiones or Warteres of Fortriu), but in order to control a larger territory, especially one as far-flung and diverse as Pictland, kings had to show presence, be constantly on the move through their kingdom, as, for instance, German kings and emperors were even in the High Middle Ages. As I mentioned, there was no system of High Kings and, as it were, sub-kings in Pictland, and the *Mormair* (from Latin *maior domus*), as an early version of earls, was a later phenomenon, probably in the eighth century, indicating a more evolved administrative structure – which, incidentally, survived into Gaelic Scotland (Alba) that continued the Pictish administrative structure.

The way to become king is better known from Dalriada and certainly Northumbria; the Celtic and Anglo-Saxon traditions were not very different in this matter. The king had to come from a dynasty with a valid claim to the succession, but he also had to bring "febas" to the table, to use the Gaelic word, loosely translated by "worth": in other words, he had to have proved himself on the battlefield, if possible. It was a unique occurrence when an eight-year-old (Osred) ascended to the Northumbrian throne in 705. Being and remaining king was a very personal matter in the early Middle Ages. The other nobles had to be kept on side, and for this the king needed a strong power base and success. In today's terms, the Pictish economy was primitive: there were no towns, no major markets, no money (the most northerly British mint was in Northumbrian York), although there will have been some long-distance trade. Few coins have been found, which will probably have been acquired and kept for their metal value.

While discussing Pictish kings, it is necessary to look briefly at the supposedly matrilineal succession on the Pictish throne, which goes back to Bede's mythical description of the origin of the Picts. This has generally been accepted, not, of course, for the reasons Bede gave, but possibly as a relict of earlier customs in the pre-Celtic population in Scotland. It does not mean that Pictish society was matriarchal – the king list disabuses us of this notion describing every king as "son of" another male. But it would mean that succession, if it remained in the same family, went through brothers, sons of his mother, first cousins, sons of the sister of the king's mother, nephews, sons of his own sisters or sons of a first cousin. This is all very complicated and difficult to prove, but it was the case that around a quarter of all kings followed their brothers. There would have been advantages in terms of dynastic flexibility instead of a rigid father/son succession, with the possibility of eliminating minors or mentally retarded successors. The fact that up to the 780s no Pictish king was named as the father of a successor king speaks for the matrilineal theory, even though new research has cast some doubt on this matter. Alex Woolf assumes that the whole theory could be connected to the early seventh century kings Brude and Nechtan, who reigned successively and are the only ones defined by their mother, as "sons of Derilei". Woolf thinks that Bede might have tried to improve their legitimacy in the eyes of his Anglo-Saxon readers, particularly in the case of Nechtan who brought the Pictish church in line with the (Roman) Northumbrian church. Bede had certainly added the rider "in cases of doubt" ("ut ubi res veniret in dubium"). But all in all, the evidence for the traditional view remains fairly strong.

When we speak about the lack of sources on Pictish history, we should not omit to mention the most important class of relic, which both informs and confuses: the Pictish stones, some of which belong among the greatest works of art in early medieval Europe. As this is a very well-known subject, dealt with in many, sometimes excellent books, I will only mention them briefly here. They range, probably in a historical sequence, from rough undressed stones with carvings to very intricate carvings in sometimes deep relief on dressed slabs. It is likely that the latter did not completely replace the former, but the presence of crosses and Christian symbols on the more highly developed stones indicates a generally later provenance. We have the famous Pictish symbols whose meaning is still very much in dispute, and we have a range of very concrete images that can be purely decorative or depict everything from mythical creatures, indicating foreign influences, animals, warriors, battle scenes and, of course, the ubiquitous Christian imagery. We can learn from these what Pictish warriors looked like, how they hunted and how they fought battles – the Aberlemno cross slab has been treated as a description of the battle of Dunnichen, to which we shall return. There are also a very few Latin inscriptions that give very little away beyond names. We should always keep the Pictish art in mind, not least as an antidote against the once widespread prejudice that the Picts were a bunch of uncultured and violent brutes.

THE COMING OF CHRISTIANITY

Pictish cross slab in the Groam House Museum, Rosemarkie

There are conflicting accounts of the way Pictland was Christianised. These are likely to reflect the fact that there will have been different pathways at different times. We must also keep in mind that the official adoption of Christianity did not mean that the whole population converted in one go – it was generally the case that the rulers agreed to convert and that this filtered through the social structure only gradually, even if there was a measure of coercion from above. The church was also at all times very good at integrating older rituals and beliefs into its own body of thought and rituals – Christmas is an example for this, which places the birth of Christ at a date of a Roman festival and the winter solstice, celebrated with clearly heathen symbols like the Christmas tree.

Long before Christianity came to Pictland, Roman Britain had already been influenced if not converted, after Rome itself had turned to the Christian religion. St.Patrick, the Irish missionary, had become a Christian after pirates had abducted him to Britain. When most of Britain came under Germanic domination, large parts of the country reverted to the old heathen beliefs. When Christianity came to the Picts it could therefore only come from Ireland. We find the earliest reference in the *Pictish Chronicle* in connection with King Nechtan Morbet (or Necton), who probably ruled in the second half of the fifth century. At this point, the *Pictish Chronicle* suddenly becomes quite effusive:

> Necton morbet the son of Erip reigned for 24 years. In the third year of his rule Darlugdach the abbess of Kildare went into exile from Ireland to Britain for the sake of Christ. In the second year after her arrival Necton

24

consecrated Abernethy to God and Saint Brigid in the presence of Darlugdach who sang alleluia over that offering.

And so Necton the great, son of Wirp [Erip], king of all the Pictish provinces, offered Abernethy to Saint Brigid, until the day of judgement, together with its territories, which are positioned from the stone in Apurfeit as far as the stone near to Ceirfuill, that is Lethfoss, and from there onto the high ground as far as Athan. This is the reason for this gift. Necton living in a life of exile, when his brother Drust expelled him, went all the way to Ireland and beseeched Saint Brigid to make a request to God on his behalf. However, as she prayed for him she said: If you return to your homeland the Lord will have pity on you: you will take over the kingdom of the Picts in peace.

Nechtan is clearly a historical figure, and his brother Drust might have been the king "who ruled a hundred years and fought a hundred battles". Brigid (or Bride) was also a historical figure who lived from around 450 to 525 and was the first abbess in Ireland after Patrick. The chronology is difficult – if Nechtan and Brigid met, she must have been very young, but in a time when lives were short, careers could be made at a very young age. Nechtan may have been converted in his Irish exile, and when he ascended to the throne after his return, he may have given lands in and around Abernethy to the Irish church. The role of Darlugdach is totally unclear – either she was in exile, as the Chronicle asserts, or she may have been an emissary of the Irish church. The church was said to have been consecrated in 486, in all likelihood a wooden structure that has disappeared without trace. Abernethy certainly became one of the ecclesiastical centres of Pictland, and even today's Kirk remains dedicated to Saint Bride. Because of the chronological difficulties, there has also been speculation that this story concerned a later Nechtan, but that would take Brigid and Darlugdach out of the equation.

There were various other conversion and missionary stories concerning southern Pictland, and the most important of them was that of St. Ninian. Bede mentions him in connection with the much later Columba.

> In the year of our Lord 565, when Justin the second took over the control of the Roman Empire after Justinian, there came from Ireland to Britain a priest and abbot named Columba, a true monk in life no less than habit; he came to Britain to preach the word of God to the kingdoms of the northern Picts which are separated from the southern part of their land by steep and rugged mountains. The southern Picts who live on this side of the mountains had, so it is said, long ago given up the errors of idolatry and received the true faith through the preaching of the Word by that reverend and holy man Bishop Ninian, a Briton who had received orthodox instruction at Rome in the faith and the mysteries of the truth. His Episcopal see is celebrated for its church, dedicated to St Martin where his body rests, together with those of many other saints. The see is now under English [Anglian] rule. This place which is in the kingdom of Bernicia is commonly called

Whithorn, the White House, because Ninian built a church of stone there, using a method unusual among the Britons.

Ninian is also a mysterious figure about whom there is no agreement among modern historians. The name occurs in a later "Life" written in the twelfth century, by the abbot Ailred from the Rievaulx monastery in Yorkshire who talks about Ninian's mission in Pictland, but in the fifth century. However, remains found in Whithorn have been dated to the sixth century, which would validate St Patrick's statement that the Picts were still heathens in the fifth century. Even Ninian's name is not certain – there was a Uinniau, who was later venerated in southwest Scotland, or a Nyniau, who was said to have done missionary work north of the Forth-Clyde line. Whether these two principal stories, about Nechtan and Brigid and about Ninian, can be reconciled is questionable, although not impossible, but one thing seems clear and corresponds with Bede's statement: the southern Picts were converted earlier to Christianity than their northern brethren, which makes absolute sense in the context of their geographical position.

With St Columba (Columcille in Irish), we enter much firmer territory. There is no doubt that he was a historical personality, one who still enjoys worldwide fame, not least through his association with Iona. We have a *Life*, written by one of his successors as abbot on Iona, Adomnan, who lived around 628 to 704. It is a typical saint's biography, full of miracles, visions and predictions, but it contains enough information to make it one of the most important sources of its time, not least about life as lived in an early medieval monastery on a small Scottish island. According to Adomnan, Columba died on June 5th, 597, and Bede reports that he was 77 years old (75 according to the Irish annals), which means that he was born around 521. He came from one of the most important Irish clans, the Uí Néill (sons of Niall) from which several Irish royal families were descended. No other founder of a sixth-century monastery had such a high birth. Adomnan claimed he was destined for the church from early childhood, but that is extremely unlikely in view of the still heathen connections of the most powerful Uí Néill. Adomnan also writes that Columba had already founded two monasteries in Ireland, which is also uncertain.

But we do know that he left Ireland when he was around forty, not a young man any more by the time's standards, and sailed to Britain to be a pilgrim for Christ, as Adomnan describes it, which led to the foundation of the monastery on Iona. This was not entirely unusual, but the circumstances of Columba's journey have raised a number of questions. He was clearly involved in Irish politics, whether in a spiritual function or as a noble of the Uí Néill is not clear. Adomnan dates Columba's voyage two years after the battle of Cúl Drebene, in which Columba is said to have played a decisive role, either by intervening through prayers in favour of the victorious northern Uí Néill, as the *Annals of Ulster* report, or by using prayers to disperse a fog, which heathen druids had created to hide the opposing army led by King Diarmait mac Cerbaill of the southern Uí Néill – this was a later version in the *Annals of Tigernach*. In various later medieval tales, his voyage to Iona had become penance for intervening in the battle and causing so many deaths – or even causing the battle itself. A more likely story is also hinted at by Adomnan, who says that Columba had been excommunicated at the Synod of Teltown, which took place in 562 and was in the sphere of influence of the defeated king of the southern Uí Néill. It is therefore likely that Columba's exile had entirely political reasons, based on the tensions between the various branches of the Uí Néill. He was said to have vowed never to return to Ireland, although in reality, he did: the famous monastery at Durrow was founded from Iona, and he participated in a meeting between the king of Dalriada and the leader of the northern Uí Néill at Derry, among other things. He remained highly honoured in his homeland, whatever the circumstances of his departure.

In a clear biblical allusion, Columba arrived on Iona with twelve comrades and is said to have been given the island by the king of Dalriada, Conall mac Comgaill, whom he is likely to have visited in the main fortress of the region, Dunadd, to seek permission and protection – although Bede writes that Iona (Hy in Gaelic) was a Pictish gift, as he had converted the Pictish king to Christianity immediately after his arrival. This would contradict the traditional timeline, and Iona was also clearly within the Scottish sphere of influence in which the Picts brought to bear their power only much later. In the following years and decades, Columba founded a number of further monasteries, starting with one on the island of Hinba as early as 574; Hinba has never been identified. In the end, there was a whole network of monasteries, including some on the Hebrides. This necessitated much travelling, not easy for an ageing man like Columba, but communication by sea was quite normal at the time. Conversely, there were also many visitors to

Iona, men seeking exile from Irish politics and pilgrims. Soon there were also Picts among the monks on Iona.

Columba's most famous journey and meeting, lovingly described by Adomnan, involved the Pictish king Brude (or Bridei), son of Maelchon. He became king in 554, around half a century after the above-mentioned Nechtan. We know almost nothing about the shadowy figures between those two; there is only an anecdote about one of the Drusts in an Irish tale: the king of the North Britons had sent his daughter Drusticc to Whithorn to be taught by the abbot Mugint, but she had instead fallen in love with a younger monk. St Finnian of Molville, who resided there, had tried to mediate, but Mugint was so angry that even Finnian's life was in danger. No more words about Drusticc, but in another story we hear about a Dustric, daughter of Trust, who had been the mother of a saint named Lonan in Galloway – if there was any truth in this, the names were too similar to be accidental. But it tells us nothing about Drust himself beyond the possible fact that he had connections well beyond Pictland. Those connections are also a possibility in the case of Brude himself. His father's name, Maelchon, does not really fit into Pictland but could indicate a link to Wales, because in its Latin version, Maglocunus, it describes a Briton king in Gwynedd, characterised as a ruthless tyrant by Gildas, the mightiest king in Britain at the time, a man of shameless immorality, despite the fact that he was a Christian. His Welsh name was Maelgwn, and he died in 547 during a plague epidemic. Was he Brude's father? He might have spent some time in Pictish exile; the name certainly occurs only twice in early medieval Britain: in Gwynedd and as Brude's father.

Brude might thus have had a very interesting dynastic connection, and Bede describes him as a very powerful king. From his reign dates the first recorded military conflict between Picts and Scots (there might have been earlier ones, of which we know nothing, but there are also reports of joint campaigns, for instance during the so-called Barbarian Conspiracy), and this set a pattern with a Pictish victory. The Irish annals speak, for the year 559, of Scots fleeing from Brude, son of Maelchon, king of the Picts, and the death of Gabran, son of Domgart – obviously the result of a battle or campaign that saw Brude and his Picts victorious. For fifteen years, no more fighting was recorded which indicates that the victory was decisive and the Scots were paying tribute. And from Adomnan's report about Columba's visit we learn that hostages from Orkney were held at Brude's court – they would have guaranteed good behaviour by a conquered territory and the prompt payment of tribute.

This brings us to Columba's famous journey to the court of King Brude, which, we believe, was near today's Inverness; it makes sense in view of Columba's route north through the Great Glen, which was the only feasible passage from Iona and Argyll/Dalriada. The king's residence is traditionally placed on the hill of Craig Phadraig, which, indeed, has a vitrified fort on its flat top, although it sits on the "wrong" side of the river Ness in relation to the Pictish heartland of today's Moray. The large fortress at Burghead was undoubtedly more important. But we can accept that Columba met the king near Inverness, because Adomnan's description of a journey through the Great Glen (with a first sighting of a "monster" at

Loch Ness) can be accepted. The date, however, is uncertain – both Adomnan and Bede describe several journeys by Columba into Pictland, even across the hills of Druim Alban. During the journey itself, several miracles are ascribed to Columba, as when he bids the monster to retreat or raises a man from the dead. This is all part of the hagiographic character of the "Life", but when he finally reaches the king, Adomnan mixes a description of miracles with an interesting confrontation with a druid named Broichan, whom he describes as Brude's foster-father, symbolising an important clash of cultures. In the fight between Columba's miracles and Broichan's magic, Columba is, of course, victorious, as when Broichan tries to prevent Columba's departure by raising a dense fog and strong headwind on Loch Ness and Columba prevails through the power of prayer.

It is difficult to accept this story of Brude's conversion to Christianity (because this is what is supposed to have happened) at face value, quite apart from its embellishment with the standard miracle stories of saints' Lives. We can assume that in the seventy years since Nechtan Morbet, Pictland had split into its main constituents, a Christian south and a heathen north. Brude seems to have reunited the two territories, but this was, realistically, only possible under Christian auspices. As mentioned, he came to power in 554, although there was at least one rival at the time, i.e. the transition might not have been peaceful. He was clearly brought up in the traditional beliefs, whether his father was a Christian Welsh king or not, because the description of the druid Broichan as his foster-father makes no sense otherwise. Broichan clearly remained a crucial figure at his court, but he must have been quite old, which would tally with Adomnan's story of his illness. The *Pictish Chronicle*, which one has to take with a very large pinch of salt, tells us that Brude was converted in the eighth year of his reign – but in 562 Columba was still in Ireland. It certainly would indicate that Brude was already a Christian when Columba came to Inverness and that Broichan was much more than a druid, perhaps a "first minister". Columba's journey to Inverness would then have been much more in the character of an official visit – in the Ionan church, Columba had very much the same function that the Pope had in the Roman church. It is, anyway, highly unlikely that Columba could have turned up unannounced, expecting to get a hearing from the mightiest king in northern Britain. It is, incidentally, quite possible that Brude had been baptised by Columba, but he would have had to travel to Ireland to do this, which is not unthinkable. This could then confirm Bede's report that Iona was a Pictish gift to Columba, despite being situated in the Scottish sphere of influence.

At that point, Brude was at the height of his power, had been able to unify the Pictish kingdom, certainly including Orkney, and also held the overlordship over Dalriada, with the Scots probably paying tribute. It was not to last. When the Scottish king Conall died, he was succeeded by his cousin, Aedan mac Gabrain, consecrated by Columba in a ceremony on Iona, described by Adomnan. He immediately pursued an aggressive military policy, attacked Orkney, which demonstrated the Scots' strength as a seafaring nation, and invaded the territory of the Miathi (Maeatae, as the Romans called them), who lived roughly between Glasgow/Edinburgh and Stirling. Adomnan mentions a battle against the Miathi, won by Aedan, who, however, suffered considerable losses, two sons and altogether 303 dead. Brude died in 584 and was succeeded by Gartnait, who still had to fight Aedan's Scots and defeated them heavily in Circinn, today's Angus. This happened around 600, and it was Aedan's last battle with the Picts. But Aedan was not finished. According to Bede, he marched against the Bernician (Anglian) king Aethilfrith, with, as he says, an immensely strong army. But at Desagstan, the Scots were beaten, fled home with few survivors, as Bede graphically noted. But Aethilfrith's brother, Theobald, also fell together with all his soldiers. Aedan died in 609, aged 74, and it is astonishing that he should have led an army at this unusually high age for an early medieval king. There were no more Scottish adventures in Northumbria. The Picts will have profited indirectly from their rivals' losses. At that point, they were not directly involved, but that was to change very soon.

FATAL RIVALS: THE PICTS AND NORTHUMBRIA

The Angles in Northumbria had founded two kingdoms, Bernicia in the north (its "capital" was Bamburgh castle), bordering on the British kingdom of Manau Gododdin around Edinburgh, and Deira in the south. Aethilfrith was the first king to unify the two parts, encouraged by his victory against the Scots. He deposed Edwin, who was a relative, but Edwin finally gained the support of the powerful East Anglian king Redwald and defeated Aethilfrith, whereupon he took over the throne. Northumbria's history is complicated and violent – to go further into it is beyond the scope of this book, although we shall meet Anglian kings at various points in the narrative. But it was Edwin, who after Redwalds death, found recognition as the strongest king in Britain ("Bretwalda") and who pushed the Northumbrian Angles into the neighbourhood of Pictland. In the late sixth century, the Northumbrians had already defeated Manau Gododdin – a battle celebrated in the epic poem *Y Gododdin* by the (Welsh) bard Aneurin, who numbered Pictish warriors among Gododdin's war-bands – and a few decades later Gododdin disappeared from the map; the Northumbrians were in today's Edinburgh. Edwin was one of the most effective kings in Northumbrian history – he established a remarkable degree of internal peace and converted to Christianity, the Roman, not the Ionan version. He got rid of potential enemies by sending them into exile, among them three sons of Aethilfrith. Eanfrith, who was the eldest, went to the Pictish court where he married a Pictish princess, who gave him a son, whereas his two younger brothers found exile in Dalriada.

In Pictland, Gartnait was succeeded in around 600 by Nechtan, grandson of Uerb. This particular Nechtan was surrounded by some confusion, because there has been speculation whether he was a Pict at all or possibly a Briton from Strathclyde, which in the early seventh century also had a king Nechtan. Was he the same person, especially as their reigns more or less coincided? It seems unlikely. But the Pictish king Brude, who defeated the Angles in 685, was celebrated in a Gaelic poem as having fought for the inheritance of his grandfather, Nechtan, king of Strathclyde, who was succeeded by Brude's father Bili. We must assume that this Bili married a Pictish princess, and Brude reached the throne in matrilineal succession. The story of the two Nechtans was probably a coincidence, and the meagre sources are not particularly helpful.

The Pictish Nechtan died in 620 and was succeeded by Kenneth (Ciniod), son of Lutren, who must have felt that the presence of a Northumbrian prince in his realm might one day become an important political card. Eanfrith was baptised, in the Pictish, i.e. Ionan church, as were the two younger princes in Dalriada. Eanfrith's son was also a potential Pictish king, as the line went through his Pictish mother, and precisely this is what happened: Talorcan ascended the Pictish throne in the 650s, albeit for only four years. It appears that the relations between Pictland and Dalriada were friendly in this period, or at least stable, and that might have been one reason why Edwin in Northumbria did not move against his potential rivals. An alliance between Picts and Scots would have been formidable, even for the most powerful ruler in Britain.

Peace and stability did not last long. Dalriada entered a period of internecine conflict, after the death of King Eoachaid Buidhe in 630, and almost simultaneously the peace in Northumbria was shattered. In 633, Edwin was heavily defeated by a coalition of the great Mercian king, Penda, and Cadwallon, the British king in North Wales. Edwin was killed, and Eanfrith returned immediately to claim his throne but left his wife and his son Talorcan behind in Pictavia. Northumbria had now split into its constituent parts again, Deira and Bernicia, and Eanfrith became king of Bernicia where he also renounced Christianity. He did not last long – when he tried to negotiate a peace treaty with the much-feared Cadwallon, he was ambushed and murdered. The Welsh king was now rampaging through Northumbria, killing and pillaging, but he, too, found his master, in the shape of Oswald, the elder of the two young princes who had been exiled in Dalriada. We can assume that he had the support of the Scottish king, Domhnall Brecc, possibly even with troops, when he decisively defeated Cadwallon near Hexham. Cadwallon was dead, and Oswald was able to reunify Northumbria, quickly gaining a very powerful position. He also invited monks from Iona to convert the still heathen Angles to Christianity, and he established the most important monastery in north-east England: Lindisfarne. This was also the point at which Gododdin disappeared from history: in 638 the Irish annals report a siege of Etin – Din Eitin, the rock on which Edinburgh castle stands. The Votadini, as the Romans had called them, had been a much less formidable neighbour for the Picts than the Northumbrian Angles, who now occupied the fortress in today's Edinburgh.

For 638, the Irish annals also mention another battle between the Scots under Domhnall Brecc and the Picts, in "Glend Mairison" (or Mureson), ending with a Pictish victory. This place is generally identified as Glen Moriston. The Scottish king conducted an aggressive military policy, but his end came four years later in a battle against the Britons of Strathclyde by the river Carron near Falkirk. As far as the Picts are concerned, we know very little about the two decades after Kenneth's death – there were three kings between around 633 and 653, all sons of a Wid (also Gwid, Guid or Foith): Gartnait, Brude and Talorc. Brude was probably the victor in Glen Moriston. As already mentioned, in 653 Eanfrith's son Talorcan became Pictish king, and he concluded yet another war with Dalriada by defeating the Scots in Strathyre in today's Perthshire – two Scottish princes were among the dead. Meanwhile, the period of stability in Northumbria had come to a cataclysmic end, when Oswald was defeated by the mighty Mercian king Penda, probably in the English Midlands; the king himself fell, was hacked to pieces, which were stuck on wooden posts to be publicly exhibited. Northumbria split again, more or less dependant on Penda. The *Historia Brittonum*, which is generally rather unreliable, speaks of huge tribute payments by Oswiu, Oswald's brother, who had become king of Bernicia, to Penda in Iudeu, which has been brought in connection with today's Stirling. This refers to the time before Talorcan and seems altogether rather unlikely. It would mean an involvement of the Strathclyde Britons in the conflict between Mercians and

Northumbrians and would have placed the Picts right at the edge of the conflict. But there are no hints regarding a Pictish involvement. When Talorcan ascended the throne it meant that the Bernician king was his uncle, but no Pictish help against Penda was forthcoming. Oswiu did not need it either, because he had already reunified Northumbria, by having his rival Oswine killed, and in 654 he managed to defeat Penda decisively near Leeds. The Mercian king was dead, and Oswiu was the mightiest ruler in Britain, recognised as Bretwalda.

For a few years, Oswiu ruled directly in the Mercian territories, introduced Christianity, but then he seems to have turned against the Picts, whether during Talorcan's rule, who, after all, was his nephew and died in 657, or during that of his successor, Gartnait, son of Donald (Donuel, Donnel), we do not know, but Bede claims that Oswiu had also subjected the largest part of the Pictish people to the rule of the Anglians (the English translation uses the word "English", which is somewhat misleading). For a short time, Oswiu's power ranged from Pictland to the Thames, which was probably the closest early medieval Britain came to a unified political entity. But there are big question marks regarding the Northumbrian dominance over the Picts. The latter cannot have been helped by the fact that their kings during the period had only short reigns – Gartnait died in 663 – and are likely to have been rather weak, despite their battle successes against Dalriada. It seems unlikely that the Northumbrians had established direct rule over a sizeable part of Pictland. They might have pushed their border further into Pictish territory, but apart from that, it was probably more a question of receiving tributes and exerting indirect influence. And this was undoubtedly restricted to the southern parts of Pictland, the fertile land-strip from Perth to Fife, which traditionally had been identified with Fortriu, the Pictish core area. I have already mentioned that recently, Fortriu has been placed further north, along the Moray coast, with the argument that certain sources had been interpreted incorrectly. Whatever the truth of the matter, there is no doubt that the two regions represented the Pictish core areas and the two kingdoms whenever Pictavia fragmented. In the case of any Northumbrian influence, however, it seems to be beyond doubt that it concerned the southern reaches of Pictland. The Grampian Mountains were a formidable barrier separating the two constituent parts.

We certainly have no reports of military engagements between Picts and Northumbrians during this period, and none of the short-lived kings died on the field of battle. Had the Picts become clients of the Northumbrian ruler? He would have had to allow them to act independently against Dalriada, with apparently undimmed military power. At the same time, the spiritual influence worked the other way. Oswald had already asked for a bishop from Iona to help convert his people to Christianity and had granted Aidan Lindisfarne. He even acted as an interpreter for Aidan, who spoke no Old English. Oswiu continued this mission and married a Christian princess (Eanfled), who, however, was following the Roman rites. There was also a Roman priest who became Bishop of York. All this foreshadowed an important split in the early medieval church in northern Britain which would also involve the Picts. Initially, the Northumbrians clarified the curious situation where even the royal family was celebrating Easter at different dates. This was due to changing methods of dating Easter, which was rather arbitrary anyway and linked to the Jewish Passover feast. The Celtic church had, as it were, "missed" the latest change – Easter Sunday is now the first Sunday after the first full moon after the spring equinox, but it can be much more complicated; how complicated can be judged from the fact that Ceolfrid, the abbot of Wearmouth and Jarrow, took 3,000 words to explain it to the later Pictish king Nechtan when asked to do so. The difference between the two dates in the Roman and the Ionan church could be up to four weeks. The other bone of contention was the monks' tonsure, which was today's round shape in the Roman church but more in the style of a central line of hair in the Ionan church, which was becoming somewhat isolated in the matter of Easter, because the Roman dating had already advanced in Ireland.

As far as Northumbria was concerned, the matter was decided in 664 at a grand synod near today's Whitby, where the Celtic position was argued by the bishop of Lindisfarne, Colman, and the Roman dating by Wilfrid, the bishop of Ripon. Once again we have to rely on Bede's report which was heavily prejudiced in favour of the Roman position and his Anglian countryman Wilfrid. According to Bede, the decisive argument was that the true Christian had to follow St. Peter, implying that the bishop of Rome was the legitimate successor of the man to whom Christ had said that he was the rock on which he wished to build his church and that he was the man to whom he was giving the key to heaven. Colman was asked whether Columba had been given a similar authority, which he could not claim. Whereupon the king declared that the matter was decided – Colman returned to Ireland, via Iona, and founded the monastery on the island of Inishboffin. Oswiu, who had managed to unify his kingdom not just politically, but now also spiritually, received great praise from the pope, who sent a golden key to his queen. Picts and Scots, however, saw themselves isolated from the mainstream of Christianity. Iona had shifted further towards the margins.

Meanwhile in Pictland, Garnait had been followed by his brother, Drust, and under his reign a lengthy conflict between the Picts on the Isle of Skye and Dalriada seems to have ended, with the result that Skye came under the control of the Gaelic Scots. This was a conflict which left some shadowy traces in the Irish annals. They speak of a war between the descendants of Aedan mac Gabrain and a certain Gartnait in 649, and for the year 668 we have the cryptic story that Gartnait's sons had travelled to Ireland with the people of Skye, which sounds highly unlikely and has been linked to the "History of Cano", an Irish tale from the ninth century, involving a love triangle between Cano, who was supposed to be Gartnait's son, an Irish girl named Cred and her older husband. Cano had come to Ireland, because he and his father had been conquered and suppressed by Aedan mac Gabrain on Skye – but Aedan was Gartnait's father, and he killed him. It all makes very little sense – Gartnait would have been a Gael, despite his Pictish name, and Cano, whose name is also not Gaelic, reappears in Welsh as Ceneu, a sixth-century British king. Perhaps Cano was the last Pictish sub-ruler on the Isle of Skye, but this is all very tenuous. All we can assume is that Skye had shifted into the Scottish sphere of influence.

When Oswiu died in 670, Drust was still on the Pictish throne. Oswiu, one of the most successful kings of his time, was succeeded by Ecgfrith, a young man in his twenties, whose fate became closely involved with that of the Picts. He inherited a vast kingdom and was soon challenged in the north where his position was possibly at its weakest. Within a year or two of his accession to the throne the Picts began to stir. Drust pushed into the area under Northumbrian control – this is also the first time that the name Fortriu occurs, obviously applied to southern Pictland to which it was attributed originally. Ecgfrith reacted immediately and led a strong army into Pictland. We have a very tendentious report on this campaign, in the Life of Wilfrid by a monk called Eddius Stephanus (or Stephen of York), which contains the only information we have about this war:

> For in his early years, while the kingdom was still weak, the bestial tribes of the Picts had a fierce contempt for subjection to the Saxon and threatened to throw off from themselves the yoke of slavery; they gathered together innumerable tribes from every nook and corner in the north, and as a swarm of ants in the summer sweeping from the hills heap up a mound to protect their tottering house. When King Ecgfrith heard this, lowly as he was among his own people and magnanimous towards his enemies, he forthwith got together a troop of horsemen, for he was no lover of belated operations; and trusting in God like Judas Maccabaeus

and assisted by the brave sub-king, Beornhaeth, he attacked with his little band of God's people an enemy host which was vast and moreover concealed. He slew an enormous number of the people, filling two rivers with corpses, so that, marvellous to relate, the slayers, passing over the rivers dry foot, pursued and slew the crowd of fugitives; the tribes were reduced to slavery and remained subject under the yoke of captivity until the time when the king was slain. (Eddius Stephanus, *The Life of Bishop Wilfrid*, Cambridge UP 1985, pp. 41-3)

While Stephen wrote this roughly fifty years after the event, the "Battle of Two Rivers" in 671 was undoubtedly decisive for more than a decade. The two rivers are most likely the Earn and Tay, which run parallel for a time, and although the description of a dam of corpses will have been vastly exaggerated, we can assume that the Picts suffered heavy losses at the hands of the Northumbrian horsemen, whose numerical inferiority will also have been exaggerated by Stephen. But his description also seems to indicate that Drust could call upon the reserves of the whole of Pictland for his rebellion against Northumbrian dominance. Now the Picts will have resumed their tribute payments to their southern neighbours, not in money, of course – there was none in Pictland – but in cattle and other agricultural and possibly craft produce.

Drust did not last very long after this disastrous loss – he was soon deposed and banished, by whom and where is unknown. But it cannot be entirely surprising; kings were expected to lead their armies in battle and often died in losing encounters. Drust survived, and his conduct of the war may have been questionable. There is also a theory that he was a Northumbrian client king who had already been deposed at the time of the battle, but this is not supported by any sources and therefore seems unlikely. He was succeeded by Brude (or Bridei), son of Bili (or Beli). The latter was not a Pictish lord but had, in all likelihood, been king of the Britons of Strathclyde, based on the fortress of Alt Clut near Dumbarton. I had already mentioned a poem celebrating the battle of Dunnichen, in which Brude's grandfather is alluded to, possibly Nechtan map Guithno, who was Bili's father. There is another intriguing story: the ninth-century *Historia Brittonum* – which, like all histories of the time, is somewhat unreliable – claims that Brude and Ecgfrith were "fratueles", meaning cousins, the sons of two brothers or sisters. Which raises the question whether Brude had any Pictish blood in his veins! If they were really related, we can assume, however, that their kinship was somewhat more remote than cousins. If this was the case, Ecgfrith will have assumed that Brude would cause him few problems, especially as the Picts were bound to take time to recover from their crushing defeat at the two rivers.

Before we hear any more about Brude, who was around twenty years older than Ecgfrith, the Northumbrian king suffered contrasting fates in his relationship with Mercia. Initially, he was able to strengthen his position by defeating Penda's son Wulfhere, who had attacked him on his own territory and, as a consequence, had to pray tribute. But only until 679, when Ecgfrith was beaten in a major battle at the river Trent by Wulfhere's brother and successor Aethelred. Among the dead was his brother Aelfwini, who had governed under Ecgfrith in

Deira, and while losing his influence in Mercia, Ecgfrith was now able formally to unify the Northumbrian kingdom – in Bede's terminology: "regnum Nordanhymbrorum". The setback in the south will have not gone unnoticed in Pictland. At the same time, a restructuring of the English church hierarchy through Theodore of Canterbury impacted on the Picts. Bernicia was split into three bishoprics, the most northerly of which was in Abercorn on the southern bank of the river Forth, which was Northumbrian territory. Bishop Trumwine, who was the rather unfortunate incumbent, was not only in charge of the spiritual well-being of the Anglian settlers but also of the Picts who were subject to English rule, as Bede describes it. And this diocese was understood to reach far into genuinely Pictish territory, to Fife and almost to Perth. This would have caused bad blood, as a visible symbol of defeat and interference in the Ionan Pictish church constitution.

While Brude will have undoubtedly done his duty towards his Northumbrian overlord, he began to consolidate his own rule in Pictland, through successful military operations in the further reaches of his territory. In the years 680-3 he attacked the fortress of Dunnottar south of Aberdeen (as noted in the *Annals of Ulster*), he led an expedition to the Orkney Isles ("deletae sunt a Bruide") and he attacked Dundurn on the bank of Loch Earn, which took him quite close to the Northumbrian sphere of influence. It is likely that this came to Ecgfrith's attention, and it is also quite possible that a newly strengthened Brude reduced or stopped tribute payments to Northumbria. Ecgfrith had just sent a controversial raiding expedition to Ireland, led by Duke Berht, who burnt and pillaged, including churches and monasteries. This was in 684, and Ecgfrith's catastrophe in Pictland in 685 was interpreted as God's punishment in Bede's *Ecclesiastical History*.

In the year of our Lord 684 Ecgfrith, king of Northumbria, sent an army to Ireland under his earldorman Berht, who wretchedly devastated a harmless race that had always been most friendly to the English, and his hostile bands spared neither churches nor monasteries. The islanders resisted force by force so far as they were able, imploring the merciful aid of God and invoking His vengeance with unceasing imprecations. And although those who curse cannot inherit the kingdom of God, yet one may believe that those who were justly cursed for their wickedness quickly suffered the penalty of their guilt at the avenging hand of God. Indeed the very next year the king rashly took an army to ravage the kingdom of the Picts, against the urgent advice of his friends and particularly of Cuthbert, of blessed memory, who had recently been made bishop. The enemy feigned flight and lured the king into some narrow passes in the midst of inaccessible mountains; there he was killed with the greater part of the forces he had taken with him, on 20 May, in the fortieth year of his age and the fifteenth of his reign. As I have said, his friends urged him not to undertake this campaign; but in the previous year he had refused to listen to the holy father Egbert, who had urged him not to attack the Irish who had done him no harm; and the punishment for his sin was that he would not now listen to those who sought to save him from his own destruction. (Bede, IV, 26)

This story needs some unravelling. While the motives for the Irish expedition are indeed entirely obscure, there will have been good reason for marching into Pictland. As we have seen, it must have seemed as though Brude was attempting to throw off the Northumbrian yoke. The battle itself, which has traditionally been placed near the village of Dunnichen not far from Forfar, looms large in early Scottish history. We shall see that it was crucial, but to describe it as the birth of Scotland, as it has been in the past, is vastly exaggerated. One of the reasons why Dunnichen or Nechtansmere has been identified as the site lies in the presence of the Aberlemno cross slab, which depicts a battle scene on its reverse side, including a large dead warrior at the bottom, which would indicate a fallen king (see illustration). The slab is not contemporary but might well have been carved and erected as a memorial to this turning point in Pictish history.

We can assume that Ecgfrith took an army of mounted warriors into Pictland, which will have consisted of relations and nobles and their war-bands – early medieval armies, especially cavalry troops, were not large by modern standards; we can assume that Ecgfrith rode with probably no more than 500 - 600 men. They would have moved into familiar territory, passing the scene of the Battle of Two Rivers, but they would have had to reach Stirling before being able to cross the river Forth, whereupon they turned east. This is open country today, but in those days there was more water, there were swamps and forests. Once in Strathearn and Angus, they left a trail of destruction in their wake. The battle-field was an area of lakes, bog and gentle hills – Dunnichen was identified as the Dún Nechtain from the sources, and much speculation is connected with the "Gueith Lin Garan" mentioned in the *Historia Britto-num*, Crane Lake, which is probably the same as Nechtansmere in the Germanic sources. This has traditionally been identified as Dunnichen Moss, which has long since been drained, but James Fraser thinks it more likely that it relates to Restenneth Loch, which filled nearly the whole valley in those days and which has Loch Fithie as its remainder, on the north side of the 172 metre high Green Hill. There was only a narrow and probably boggy land bridge between this lake and the neighbouring Loch of Forfar, which was much larger, too. Directly adjacent to Green Hill is the 233 metre high Dunnichen Hill and on the opposite side of the valley Turin Hill with the remains of Kemp's Castle, probably a Pictish fortress.

The carving on the Aberlemno cross slab could well represent a sequence of events, depicted in three lines, akin to an early cartoon. The Germanic warriors can be identified from their helmets with long face guards and are only shown on horse-back, while the Picts have a mixture of riders and foot-soldiers. The top row or register shows a Pictish horse-man chasing an Anglian rider, the middle row has a three-deep Pictish infantry formation fighting Anglian cavalry, with swords, a long lance and spiked shields, and the bottom row has two riders fighting each other and in the corner the dead king, picked by a raven, the bird of death. It is likely that the Picts had fortified themselves with an army perhaps three times the size of the attackers on the top of Dunnichen Hill, which rises around

100 metres above the valley floor. Brude, who was around 60 years old in 685, will have lured Ecgfrith's troop with a small raiding force on to the hill side and into the disadvantageous position of having to attack uphill. This would be shown in the top row of the Aberlemno cross slab. The Anglian riders would then have met the entrenched Pictish infantry, running up against swords, lances and spiked shields, which could be very effective against horses. This was the scene in the middle register. Either the Anglians were driven back, or the battle got bogged down, at which point the Pictish riders would have intervened and driven their enemies down the hill, towards the lakes and the boggy land. And once a medieval army was in disarray, wholesale slaughter could ensue, as it had happened to the Picts at the Two Rivers. King Ecgfrith was dead, and his knights were butchered, drowned or went into captivity, became Pictish slaves. The terrain and the distance to their homeland were such that no one will have escaped.

There is, of course, a big question mark behind the location of the battle. The gentle landscape around Forfar bears little resemblance to Bede's description of "narrow passes in the midst of inaccessible mountains". The usual argument is that Bede wrote much later and would have had an interest in making the terrain sound more forbidding and dangerous than it actually was. The description might have changed in the retelling of a story which can have reached Northumberland only indirectly, assuming none of the warriors returned home. And

Battle Scene on the Aberlemno Stone

if any did, they would have wanted to sound more heroic than they actually were. Alex Woolf has suggested a different solution. In line with his (now generally accepted) theory that Fortriu was in Moray, not in Perthshire and Angus, he raises the possibility that Ecgfrith did not turn right at Stirling but marched north across Drumochter and met the Pictish army at Dunachton in Badenoch, at the north-western end of Loch Nish where the description of the landscape as given by Bede would be much more accurate. But this seems rather unlikely to me. Even if the Pictish core area was in Moray, this does not mean that the Northumbrians had any interest in it. Their sphere of influence lay clearly in southern Pictland, and that is where they would have launched a campaign of punishment. Crossing the Grampian Mountains at the only feasible point would have been a major undertaking that even Ecgfrith would have been unlikely to attempt. Objectively, he had no reason to fear the Picts in territory where he had already won a major battle, even against the odds in terms of numbers. The fact that the outcome was different on this occasion was a big surprise. It would not have been if the Picts had attacked him in the narrow defile at Dunkeld, on the bleak hillsides of Drumochter. Or in the dense Caledonian Forest in the outer reaches of the Cairngorms. Therefore, I tend to stick with the traditional location.

The battle had major consequences. This was the first time that an Anglian king had fallen in an encounter with northern Britons. The shocked echo reverberated through the whole of Britain. Many reports say that Ecgfrith was buried on

Iona, although there is no good reason for this. The battle seems to have had great repercussions for the Northumbrian kingdom, too – Bede writes half a century later that "from this time the hopes and strength of the English kingdom began to ebb and fall away. For the Picts recovered their own land which the English had formerly held, while the Irish who lived in Britain and some part of the British nation recovered their independence, which they have now enjoyed for about forty-six years." There was no more tribute from Pictavia, Dalriada or Strathclyde. All this, one should add, rather puts previous Northumbrian defeats against Mercia, for instance, into a different perspective, because they generally had no such long-term effect. A grim fate also awaited the Anglians who had settled on Pictish territory – according to Bede they were slain, enslaved or had to flee from the Pictish lands. This included the bishop of Abercorn, Trumwine, who ended his days in the monastery at Whitby.

There is no doubt that Dunnichen represented a turning point in the history of what was to become Scotland. Whether it was as important as Bannockburn, Flodden or Culloden is not really relevant. In view of the fluctuating fates of the Germanic entities in Britain, it is by no means certain that they would have held their position in Scotland, even without this battle. But one thing is certain: there has not been direct English rule in Scotland since Dunnichen. The Anglians were never again able to cross the Clyde-Forth line. As simultaneously the remaining Celtic kingdoms in England and the future Scottish Lowlands had disappeared, like Gododdin, or came under permanent pressure, like Strathclyde, as Wales was becoming the Celtic fortress it still is today in some sense, the situation around 700 was prefiguring the shape of Britain as it has persisted, despite the huge, temporary upheaval the Vikings were to bring about.

Brude died in 693, peacefully in his own bed. He was around 70 years old, a great age for the time. His body was taken to Iona where, as the story goes, the abbot, Adomnan, author of the *Life* of Columba, kept vigil by the open coffin. At the start of dawn, the Pictish king had shown signs of life, and opened his eyes as the day began. Resurrection legends are normally the preserve of "holy" clerics, and this shows the importance of King Brude. A monk, described as a sceptic, admonished Adomnan not to go through with this – if he could waken the dead, no one could be his successor who had not the same ability. Adomnan agreed, blessed the king and let him die. If it is true that Ecgfrith was also buried on Iona, the two bitter enemies and "fratrueles" had found their final destination side by side.

CORRECTIO: THE PICTS TURN TO ROME

Brude passed a much-strengthened Pictish kingdom on to his successor Tarain, son of Entfidich, about whom we only know that he was expelled from Pictland after only four years and found exile in Ireland. He might have found an unhappy end there. In his *Life of Columba*, Adomnan mentions an exiled Pictish noble named Taran whom Columba sent to a man called Feradach, who lived on Islay, assuming he would be looked after there for a few months. Feradach, however, had him murdered treacherously only a few days after his arrival. The irate Columba punished this dastardly act by prophesying that Feradach would die soon – "in autumn when the pigs are fattened on acorns in the woods, before he has the first taste of their meat, he will be overtaken by sudden death and carried off to hell". Feradach, we hear from Adomnan, made light of this prophecy but tried to disprove it when the time came by getting some fresh meat into his mouth as quickly as possible, but before he could get a morsel between his teeth, he fell down and died. The fact that this episode is attributed to Columba should not worry us: historical time was a relative concept in early medieval writing, and Adomnan could well have referred to a contemporary event, because it fitted into his description of the saint.

Tarain was followed by yet another Brude, son of Derilei, his mother. Her female sex has only recently been established, and despite the theory of matrilineal succession, it was unusual that the mother's name was used. However, his father, Dagart, was probably a Scot, chief of the clan Cenél Comgaill, which meant that Brude was of mixed Scottish and Pictish origin. His claim to fame was that he signed the "Law of the Innocents" (or "Adomnan's Law"), which was a remarkable achievement in the early Middle Ages. As the name says, it was formulated by Adomnan and proclaimed in the Irish town of Birr in either 696 or 697. The core passage, on the protection of children and clerics from war, of *Cain Adamnain, An Old-Irish Treatise on the Law of Adamnan*, says:

> This is the enactment of Adamnan's Law in Ireland and Britain: exemption of the Church of God with her people and her emblems and her sanctuaries and all her properties, live and dead, and her law-abiding laymen with their lawful wives who are obedient to Adamnan and to a lawful, wise and pious confessor. The enactment of this Law of Adamnan is a perpetual law on behalf of clerics and women and innocent children until they are capable of slaying a man, and until they take their place in the tribe, and their (first) expedition is known.

The long list of signatories includes the Pictish king, Brude, and Bishop Curetan of Rosemarkie, who was probably the Pictish primate at the time and who was in all likelihood the "real" St. Boniface, who is celebrated as the bringer of Christianity to the local area. If he himself took on the name Bonifatius, it might indicate that he had sympathies for the church of Rome and might have influenced developments in Pictland in that direction. Despite Brude's name on the list, historians think that he might not have gone to Ireland in person, being represented by the influential Curetan instead. Other signatories were the king of Dalriada and more than 50 Irish kings. The law was renewed in 730 and carried drastic punishments for transgressions, but not a single case is known where such punishments were carried out. It was probably more than anything else a remarkable gesture in what is still know as the "dark ages".

In 698, just after the proclamation of Adomnan's Law, Brude fought another battle against the Northumbrians, in which the leader of the Anglian army, Berctred, was killed. It was clearly another Pictish victory, although the annalists give us no details, including the site of the battle. But it will have consolidated the Pictish gains at Dunnichen, perhaps including the integration of Manau, the territory between Stirling and Edinburgh, into the Pictish kingdom (Pictavia, in the Latin sources of the time). Brude might have been the first Pictish king to control all territory right down to the old Antonine Wall between Glasgow and Edinburgh, which for a short period had marked the furthest extent of Roman rule in Britain.

With the turn of the century, we enter a period which eventually led to a remarkable rapprochement between Pictavia and Northumbria. It began with a – for the time – remarkable king: Ecgfrith's successor in Northumbria, his brother Aldfrith, whose legitimacy was based on his descent from Oswiu. He was never in his life actively involved in a battle, and we can assume that the war in which Brude defeated the Northumbrians was not started by Aldfrith, although it is quite possible that Berctred acted on his own accord. Before ascending to the throne, Aldfrith had been a monk on Iona; he was described as "wise" by the Iona chronicle, as "doctissimus" (most learned) by Bede and as "most wise" by Stephanus. Despite this reputation as a philosopher king, Aldfrith managed to stabilise his kingdom, which, however, unravelled rather quickly after his death in 704. Out of this, another unusual situation emerged: after a short interval, a minor, eight-year-old Osred, became Northumbrian king, until he was killed in Mercia in 716, under unknown circumstances. It should also be mentioned that in the same year as Aldfrith, Adomnan, the abbot of Iona, died, at the age of around 76. Iona could have done with his leadership in subsequent years.

Brude survived both these men by only two years, and he was followed by his brother Nechtan (Pictish: Naiton), who was thus also the son of Derilei and who was one of the best-documented Pictish kings, not least through Bede's narration, who was now writing about his own time (he had been inaugurated into priesthood in 703). While Nechtan's reign did not overlap with Aldfrith's, they had something in common: within early medieval limits, both could be described as "intellectuals". But while Aldfrith's reign was largely peaceful, Nechtan was soon involved in serious military conflicts. In the *Annals of Ulster* for 709 we read about a victorious battle "against the men of Orkney", in which "Arablair's son fell". Nechtan may have put down a rebellion on this distant Pictish island territory. For the following year, the same annals report an internal conflict in Dalriada, among the Cenél Comgaill, "in which two sons of Nechtan, son of Dargata, were killed". It is tempting to assume that those were sons of the Pictish king, who would have been involved indirectly, and that Dargata was Brude's and Nechtan's father, the husband of Derilei. This might then point to a weakening of the Pictish influence among the Scots – or if

Dargata was, indeed, a Scot, it might have been, at least partly, an internal affair in Dalriada.

The year 711 saw the next instalment of the intermittent wars between the Picts and the Northumbrian Angles. This time the Picts suffered a heavy defeat, "a slaughter of the Picts by the Saxons in Mag Manonn, where Finnguine son of Deile Roith met an untimely death." The fact that the *Annals of Ulster* use the name Saxons should not worry us – Saxons and Angles were often not differentiated. As the battle took place in "Mag Manonn", we can assume that it was a Pictish attack – Mag Manonn was the old Manau where the British kingdom of Gododdin had been, i.e. around Edinburgh, which had been conquered by the Northumbrians. The Picts were thus clearly outside their own territory; it could well be that they were trying to test the mettle of the young Northumbrian king. The victorious Anglian army was led by Beorhtfrith, a relative of Beorhtred, who had been killed in 698, in the defeat against the Picts. This could indicate that the Northumbrian kings had handed the defence of their northern border to one family, and Finnguine might have played a similar part on the Pictish side, which would have meant that neither king was involved directly, certainly not the minor on the Northumbrian throne. To conclude the dramatic events of these war-torn years, Dalriada inflicted a heavy defeat on the Britons of Strathclyde in the same year, at a place called Lorg Ecclet, which has not been identified. Only six years previously, the Scots had suffered a similarly heavy defeat against the same opponents.

It was all the more surprising and much more in keeping with the probably most highly educated of all Pictish monarchs that Nechtan executed a complete turnaround towards the Northumbrians in the same year, 711. This concerned the unsatisfactory religious split that had developed in the British Isles, not least since the Synod of Whitby in 664, which had unified the Northumbrian church on the basis of the Roman rite. Nothing was likely to change while the powerful figure of Adomnan was alive, but there are indications that the Ionan church had already lost some of its influence. Bishop Curetan might have had Roman sympathies, and there were even some stirrings on Iona itself, if we can believe some vague hints by Bede, who points to an Anglian monk named Egbert who had been urging reformation, and even the new abbot, Dunchadh, was said to have Roman tendencies. Virtually out of the blue, Nechtan took a step that became known as "correctio" – the correction of religious errors. It is worth quoting Bede on this matter.

> At that time Nechtan, king of the Picts, who lived in the northern parts of Britain, having been convinced by his assiduous study of ecclesiastical writings, renounced the error which he and his race had until then held about the observation of Easter, and led all his people to celebrate with him the catholic time of keeping the Lord's resurrection. In order to make the change more easily and with greater authority, he sought help from the English who, he knew, had long since based their religious practices on the example of the holy Roman and apostolic Church. So he sent messengers to the venerable Ceolfrith, abbot of the monastery of the apostles St Peter and St Paul, one part of which stands

at the mouth of the river Wear and the other part near the river Tyne in a place called Jarrow. ... The king asked the abbot to send him information by letter to enable him to confute more convincingly those who presumed to celebrate Easter at the wrong time; also about the shape and method of tonsure by which it was fitting that clerics should be distinguished: notwithstanding this request he himself had no small measure of knowledge on these matters. He also asked for builders to be sent to build a church of stone in their country after the Roman fashion, promising that it should be dedicated in honour of the blessed chief of the apostles. He also said that he and all his people would always follow the customs of the holy Roman and apostolic Church, so far as they could learn them, remote though they were from the Roman people and from their language. Abbot Ceolfrith complied with his pious wishes and requests, sending the builders he asked for and also a letter couched in the following terms ...

And there follows the longest document Bede quotes in his *Ecclesiastical History*, presumably because he himself was involved in writing it. After the document, he continues:

When this letter had been read in the presence of King Nechtan and many learned men and carefully translated into his own language by those who were able to understand it, it is said that he was greatly delighted by the exhortation; so he rose in the midst of the company of his assembled leaders, and knelt down, thanking God for having made him worthy to receive such a gift from England. 'Indeed,' he said, 'I knew before that this was the true observance of Easter, but I now understand the reasons for observing this date so much more clearly that I seem up to this to have known far too little about it in every respect. So I publicly declare and proclaim in the presence of you all, that I will for ever observe this time of Easter, together with all my people; and I decree that all clerics in my kingdom must accept this form of tonsure which we have heard to be so completely reasonable.' He at once enforced his word by royal authority also. The nineteen-year cycles for Easter were forthwith sent out by public order throughout the Pictish kingdoms, to be copied, learned, and acted upon, while the erroneous eighty-four-year cycles were everywhere obliterated. All ministers of the altar and monks received the tonsure in the form of a crown; and the reformed nation [Latin: "gens correcta"] rejoiced to submit to the newly-found guidance of Peter, the most blessed chief of the apostles, and to be placed under his protection. [*Ecclesiastical History*, V.21]

What was really meant by this "correctio" has puzzled historians. We can accept that Nechtan did turn to Northumbria for advice, specifically to Ceolfrith, who was the most learned cleric in that kingdom, that he did receive a letter and took the measures mentioned by Bede. But the rest should be treated with some caution.

There is, of course, the possibility that Nechtan was guided precisely by the reasons Bede ascribed to him – he may have been convinced by the arguments and by his Christian mission as a king. He knew that Northumbria had adopted the Roman rite forty years previously and he may have felt that opinion was shifting in his own kingdom, perhaps decisively so. Subsequent events show that it could be seen to be in his interest to weaken the influence of Iona, which after all was in the Scottish sphere of influence, and his own position vis a vis Dalriada had been weakened of late. Nechtan's own personal development at a later stage points to a certain degree of religious motivation. On the other hand, the "correctio" could have been motivated more by political than religious considerations. He had just lost a major battle against the Northumbrians, but with a minor on the throne, the southern neighbour itself was not in a position of real strength. It was a good time for a peace overture which, for all we know about Nechtan, was in tune with his own inclination. With the approach to Ceolfrith, he had opened a diplomatic channel, which was accepted with alacrity. And, indeed, shortly afterwards some kind of political arrangement between the two states was concluded – Bede called it a peace treaty ("foedus pacis"), which was still in force in 731, when Bede concluded his *Ecclesiastical History*. It was certainly a period of stability between the two entities.

As we have seen, Bede tried very hard to give the impression that Nechtan was in full control of the Pictish kingdom, was able to implement the new arrangement without any difficulty. It might have been the case, but there is no doubt that Nechtan had to act with a certain degree of caution – he had to avoid the impression that he subjected himself to even as little as the advice of the southern neighbour, who had just beaten him on the battle field. Would he really have knelt down in front of a lower-ranking delegation from the former enemy? The young king had not travelled to Pictavia, or otherwise Bede would have certainly mentioned it. In the Middle Ages, there was no shame attached to humbling oneself in front of God, but that would not have been the image he projected with this act, in the presence of the leading Pictish aristocrats – some of whom might even have fought at Dunnichen.

Another curiosity was the request to send stone masons from Northumbria who were asked to help with the construction of a stone church. Of course, people in Scotland had used stone as a building material for virtually thousands of years, as the hugely impressive monuments on Orkney demonstrate. The Picts had constructed fortresses from stone, too, the largest being Burghead, but perhaps they were deficient in the use of mortar. It is unclear where the resulting church stood – candidates were Meigle, Restenneth and Aberlemno, near Dunnichen. It appears that the Germanic stone masons imported another revolutionary technique into Pictland, because this was *roughly* the date when the Picts started creating the relief cross slabs – Class Two stones in the traditional terminology. Very soon, they were to surpass anything created by their Anglian mentors if this is what they were.

Whatever motivated Nechtan, it certainly put pressure on Iona if it wanted to retain its influence on Pictland or become a minor outpost attached to Dalriada. Under the influence of the above-mentioned Egbert, it finally followed the Pictish about-turn. Egbert, who was later canonised, came originally from Lindisfarne and emigrated later to Ireland where

Cross slab in Nigg church

he lived in a monastery in Rathelmigisi in Connaught. In 684 he tried in vain to dissuade Ecgfrith from his bloody invasion of Ireland (which Bede blamed for his defeat at Dunnichen) and was engaged in educating monks for missionary work in Germany. When he fell victim to the plague, he swore he would go into exile if he survived. He did and travelled to Iona where in 712 he became bishop. He led the community on Iona into acceptance of the Catholic Easter date and of the Roman tonsure. On the day of his death, 24 April 729, Easter was celebrated on Iona for the first time according to the official Roman calculation, after, it appears, a lengthy period of transition, because the abbot, Dunchadh, had executed the reform as early as 716. There must have been a lot of residual resistance against this reform among the Iona community.

As far as Nechtan was concerned, all this was too late. In 717, he ejected the "Iona Family" from his Pictish kingdom, across Druim Alban effectively into Dalriada. While it is likely that the "correctio" met no resistance among the people at large, there could have been some resistance among the Columban clerics. We should not imagine that all priests were driven out of the country; however, a number of high-profile clerics will have been forced to leave, but otherwise the action will have been largely symbolic – a change of authority, undoubtedly with political overtones. Nechtan seems to have succeeded in uniting the whole of the Pictish kingdom with its fissiparous tendencies, and having a home-grown spiritual authority could only bolster his position. There was some danger associated with that: it could create the impression that the influence of Iona was replaced by that of Lindisfarne, of the old enemy's church, but it appears that the Picts were quite capable of developing their own religious centres.

We know about some of the major ecclesiastical centres in Pictavia, like Rosemarkie, Abercorn, St. Andrews (Kilrimont) and Dunkeld. Rosemarkie, which appears to have been the seat of the Pictish primate, certainly for some of the time, is a particularly interesting case in point because of its association with the monastery in Portmahomack. This is possibly the best-documented Pictish site, due to the excavation by a team from the University of York, led by Professor Martin Carver. It uncovered a smallish but highly structured monastic community in a well-developed settlement with workshops clearly for the production of religious goods and a vellum manufacture, which indicates that there was a scriptorium. It has been speculated that the famous *Book of Kells* might not have been written on Iona but in Portmahomack. This answers the age-old question whether the Picts were literate: they clearly were, although possibly nothing has survived, but they wrote, as everybody else did, in Latin – holy books and presumably laws. The rare inscriptions on Pictish stones point in the same direction. After 800, the monastery experienced a cataclysmic event, after which the community changed – it now contained women, too – and so did the purpose of craft production: it had been attacked and burned down by Viking raiders.

Nechtan's rule might have been undisputed through most of his reign but there was some unrest immediately after the communication with Ceolfrith, which appears to have been an attempted usurpation of his throne. When Nechtan came to power, he had two surviving brothers, Kenneth (Ciniod), son of Derilei, and Talorcan, son of Drostan, who must have been a half-brother, possibly from a second marriage of his mother. Kenneth was murdered in 713, and in the same year Talorcan was arrested, perhaps because he was suspected of being an accomplice in Kenneth's murder, who, after all, would have been Nechtan's successor as the third son of Derilei. Talorcan, who eventually was to end up in Dalriada, might have tried to get rid of a rival for the throne if he intended to topple Nechtan. But Nechtan clearly won this dynastic conflict and remained untroubled for a further decade, at least on the surface. The chaotic years after 724 could indicate that some resentment at the cultural influence from south of the border had started to build.

In 724, Nechtan suddenly gave up his throne and retreated into a monastery. Was this a voluntary act of a roughly 60-year-old man who had the reputation of being learned and pious? This was, after all, not unique in the early Middle Ages – only twenty years previously, Aethilred, king of Mercia, had given up his throne in favour of Coenred and became abbot. Coenred himself then gave up his kingdom for "the sake of the Lord". On the other hand, Nechtan might have been forced from the throne and into a monastery. His position was taken by a Drust, about whom we have no other information, not even his father's name. Whether Drust was there by will of Nechtan or was a usurper, he did not remain unchallenged. First, in 725, his son Simul was captured by presumably a rivalling faction. A year later, Nechtan emerged from his monastery and was immediately involved in a power struggle. It is unclear whether this was an attempted comeback or whether Drust had dragged him from his monastery, but perhaps the latter, as this entry in the Ulster chronicle indicates: "Nectan son of Derile is imprisoned by king Drust." He may have assumed that Nechtan was involved in his son's abduction.

Very soon, Drust had a direct challenger, in the shape of Alpin (or Elphin), who might have been a sub-king in Atholl, which then was much larger than today's territory of that name, possibly comprising the whole area which was traditionally described as Fortriu. We know just as little about Alpin as we do about Drust. According to the *Pictish Chronicle*, he ruled jointly with Drust. That is highly unlikely: we should rather assume that Pictavia had split once again into its constituent parts, north and south. There is no record of a military confrontation between the two, but one consequence was that Nechtan was once again at liberty. He did not return to his monastery but became a major factor in the ensuing power struggle. This started in earnest in 727 or 728, when the decisive personality entered the scene: Angus, son of Fergus. This is the anglicised version of the name which I shall use – in Pictish, he was probably Oniust map Urguist and in Old Irish Oengus mac Fergusso. According to Irish genealogies, Angus came from The Mearns (today's Kincardine), and he had two brothers – Brude, who succeeded him in 761 (as "Rex Fortrenn", king of Fortriu, in the chronicles), and Talorcan, who in 736 led Pictish troops against the Scots. Angus was not a young man, because he had a son called Brude, who in 731 was old enough to lead an army. In 728, Angus must have been at least 40.

That was the year of the first major battle in the civil war, in which Angus defeated Alpin near Moncrieffe in the vicinity of Perth, killing Alpin's son and many of his supporters. The location of the battle indicates that control of southern Pictavia was at stake here. Alpin was not finished. A few months later, the rivals clashed again, but this time Angus was allied with the old king, Nechtan, and this battle was decisive – Alpin disappeared from the scene; the place of the battle is given as Caissel Credi in the *Annals of Ulster* (Castle Credi), which has not been located. The power struggle was down to three now, because the alliance between Angus and Nechtan did not last. It appears that Nechtan attempted to restore his rule after the victorious battle. The *Annals of Ulster* speak of "exactores", whom Nechtan seems to have installed, which could mean tax collectors but probably described much wider functions, as his half-brother Finnguine was among them. A battle between the two rivals was certainly unavoidable, and in 729 Angus won decisively. This is the translated entry in the *Annals of Ulster*: "The battle of Monid Carno near Loch Laegde between the hosts of Nectan and the army of Aengus, and Nectan's exactors fell i.e. Biceot son of Monet, and his son, Finnguine son of Drostan, Feroth son of Finnguine, and many others; and the adherents of Aengus were triumphant." The location of this battle is also unclear – Loch Laegde might be Loch Lochy, but Monid Carno has also been identified as the Cairn o'Mount in the Grampian Mountains. There is an alternative interpretation of this entry, by James Fraser. He translates "hostis" in the Latin source not with troops but enemy: Angus had defeated Nechtan's enemy, i.e. Drust, and the "exactores" had been the oppressors of Nechtan. In my view, this does not stand up linguistically, nor does it accord with the facts, because Nechtan was now out of the reckoning, despite the fact that he survived until 732, perhaps after retreating into a monastery for a second time.

The civil war ended in the same year, 729, with a battle between Angus and Drust, at Druim Derg Blathug, as the *Annals of Ulster* call it, once again an unknown location, because Druim Dearg, "red ridge", is particularly unspecific. Not so the result: Drust was killed, and Angus was now the undisputed ruler in Pictland. The date: Friday, 12 August 729. Angus became possibly the greatest of all Pictish kings. The *Pictish Chronicle* gives the length of his reign as thirty years, until his death in 761, which leaves the question what happened in the two years between 729 and 731. Did he grant Nechtan another two years on the throne? That is highly unlikely. It may be just an error in the Chronicle, of which there are many.

ANGUS THE GREAT

In 731 the Venerable Bede concluded his *Ecclesiastical History*, which, incidentally, also meant that we lose one of the most important sources regarding the history of northern Britain, including the Picts. His final paragraphs paint a picture of peace and prosperity, altogether untypical compared to what had passed.

> The Picts now have a treaty of peace with the English [Angles] and rejoice to share in the catholic peace and truth of the Church universal. The Irish who live in Britain [i.e. the Scots] are content with their own territories and devise no plots or treachery against the English. Though, for the most part, the Britons [Strathclyde] oppose the English through their inbred hatred, and the whole state of the catholic Church by their incorrect Easter and their evil customs, they cannot obtain what they want in either respect. For although they are partly their own masters, yet they have also been brought partly under the rule of the English.

> In these favourable times of peace and prosperity, many of the Northumbrian race ["race" is always a rather awkward translation of "gens"], both noble and simple, have laid aside their weapons and taken the tonsure, preferring that they and their children should take monastic vows rather than train themselves in the art of war. What the result will be, a later generation will discover.

This is the state of the whole of Britain at the present time, about 285 years after the coming of the English to Britain, in the year of our Lord 731. Let the earth rejoice in His perpetual kingdom and let Britain rejoice in His faith and let the multitude of isles be glad and give thanks at the remembrance of His holiness. (*Ecclesiastical History*, V.23)

Some of this was clearly wishful thinking by Bede, who died in 735, aged 63. Northumbria might have been generally peaceful but not particularly stable – after young Osred's death in 716, his successor Coenred kept the throne for only two years, to be followed by Osred's brother, Oscric, who seems to have pushed the Northumbrian borders into Galloway, at the cost of the Strathclyde Britons. In the year of his death, 729, two comets were visible, causing a great deal of concern. Coenred's brother, Ceolwulf, now became king, but he was deposed in 731 and sent into a monastery. He returned quickly, but in 737 he gave up his throne at his own volition to become a monk. It was just as well that the peace treaty with the Picts was a certain insurance against the northern neighbours exploiting this apparent weakness.

Angus meanwhile had ended the dynastic wars in Pictland, which had certainly prevented an active foreign policy, and was now the undisputed ruler in the whole of the kingdom. He began his reign under a lucky constellation, under no pressure from the south or from Dalriada, which suffered a series of dynastic conflicts, with the clans of Kintyre and Lorn as their focus – Lorn comprised the area around today's Oban and the Isle of Mull. While Nechtan ruled in Pictavia, Dalriada had King Selbach from the clan Cenél Loairn on the throne, who, like Nechtan, retreated into a monastery, in 723, after twenty years as king. This caused a period of extreme confusion. Selbach handed his crown to his son Dungal, but he kept it for only three years, when he was expelled by Eochaid mac Echdach from the clan Cenél nGabráin, which dominated Kintyre and adjacent islands like Jura and Arran. Now Selbach attempted a comeback but failed and finally died in 730. A year later, Dungal reappeared on the scene and conquered and destroyed Tairpert Boittir, today's Tarbert. It is astonishing that the thinly populated Dalriada still had enough reserves to send a fleet to Northern Ireland and conduct a successful campaign there.

But the same year, 731, introduced another factor into the politics of Dalriada: the Pictish king Angus. And he would not let go. There has been speculation why Angus focussed on Dalriada to such a degree. It could be that under the sons of Derilei, like Nechtan, who were of half-Scottish origin, the involvement in the neighbours' affairs had come to be seen as natural, that Dalriada was perhaps already seen as part of the Pictish sphere of influence, despite the fact that Nechtan had rejected Iona as the spiritual centre. But especially under Angus, this involvement had no benevolent aspects. While the Scots with their thorough military organisation were generally able to perform beyond what could be expected, were often on an equal footing with the Picts, in the shape of Angus they had an opponent who was militarily more powerful and ruthless than anyone they had encountered until then.

The first act of the war was initiated by an army led by Angus' son Brude which defeated a Scottish unit under Talorc. That was a Pictish name, which meant that his mother was either Pictish or half-Pictish – his father came from the clan Cenél nGabráin, in southern Dalriada, mainly Kintyre. He fled there, to the Scottish high king Eoachaid, who, however, was under pressure from Dungal, as we have seen. Things become very confusing now, shot through with speculation about Pictish involvement. There has been speculation that Talorc might have granted refuge to Talorcan, Nechtan's half-brother, who we last met as sub-ruler in Atholl and whom Angus hoped to get rid off, because he might have ear-marked his son Brude for the sub-kingship in Atholl. Another speculation concerns possible Pictish support for Dungal's attack on Eochaid, especially as three years later, Flaithbertach, the son of Loingsech, king of the Cenél Conaill in Irish Donegal, led a fleet from Dalriada against the rival clan Cenél nÉogain, a fleet that, according to an Irish chronicle, came from Fortriu. While Flaithbertach suffered a decisive defeat, we seem to have the intriguing situation that the Picts were heavily involved in the machinations of the various Scottish clans, possibly even in Ireland itself.

It was to become much more direct. If Angus had hoped to involve his son Brude in his government structure, perhaps build him up as a successor, he was to be disappointed, because immediately after his victory against Talorc, he retreated into an Irish monastery on Tory Island off the coast of Donegal. He was not left in peace there. In 733, Dungal led a Scottish army to Ireland, possibly as part of the war in which the allegedly Pictish fleet participated. This expedition took on the character of a raiding party – they stormed an unidentified island named Inis Cuirenrigi and in the same move, say the *Annals of Ulster*, "Dúngal son of Selbach profaned Torach [Tory Island] when he forcibly removed Bruide from it". This was not only in contravention of Adomnan's Law, which had just been renewed three years previously when his remains had been taken to Ireland, but also a colossal provocation of the Pictish king. Why? Perhaps it was connected with the fact that in Dungal's home territory, Lorn, Muiredach, son of Ainbcellach, had seized the crown. Ainbcellach had been toppled and later killed by Dungal's father, Selbach. Perhaps Dungal suspected that Angus had been instrumental in this overthrow, and he was seeking revenge.

Pictish involvement in Dalriada became more obvious in 734, when Talorc, who had been defeated by Brude in 731, was seized by his brother, clapped in chains and handed over to the Picts. The brother in question was probably Cu Bretan, son of Congus. It is unlikely that he attempted to pacify the Pictish king, by handing over one prisoner in exchange for his son, because after all, Talorc's clan had been fighting against Dungal's. It is more likely that Cu Bretan followed a request or, perhaps rather, order by Angus, who had no intention of keeping him as a hostage. He was immediately executed by ritual drowning. The same fate befell soon thereafter Talorcan, who was seized near Dunnollie, a fortress in Lorn, probably by the new king, Muiredach. He was also clapped in chains and taken to Pictland. He, too, was ritually drowned, albeit five years later. Angus had got rid of a potential rival, but it became ever clearer that Angus was a man whose word carried weight in Dalriada. It is less relevant whether he actually issued an order or whether Muiredach had anticipated what Angus might have wanted. It also gives some credence to the suspicion that Angus was involved in Muiredach's ascent to power. Still in 734, Dungal was wounded while fighting for an unidentified fortress named Dun Leithfinn and fled to Ireland, "from the power of Aengus" (*Annals of Ulster*). Within one year, Angus had now seen one enemy flee and had brought two others into his power, without having to fight a battle. It showed that nothing could happen in Dalriada without Angus' involvement. But while Dungal might have fled, Brude was still in his power.

And Dungal had not yet given up. In 736 he returned to Dalriada, and this time Angus reacted immediately, in person. For the first time since the battle of Dunnichen, a Pictish king personally led an army on a foreign expedition, in an invasion the kind of which the Scots in Dalriada had never experienced. It was a brutal campaign, in which he devastated the territories through which he marched ("uastatio"), and finally reached Dunadd in the border country between Lorn and Kintyre. Dunadd, seen as the main fortress in Dalriada, was conquered, completely destroyed and burned down – so thoroughly that the chronicles did not mention it again; archaeological research has shown that it probably remained uninhabited until around 800. Here Dungal was finally captured, so was his brother Feradach, and now finally Brude gained his freedom. He was, however, so weakened by his captivity that he died soon thereafter. The annals do not tell us what happened to Dungal – it cannot have been pleasant. Feradach was kept as a hostage in Pictavia.

While Angus finished off Dungal and Dunadd, his brother Talorcan, son of Fergus, led an army from Fortriu against Muiredach, whose anticipation of Angus' wishes was obviously no insurance policy. The location of the battle is given by the *Annals of Ulster* as "Cnoc Cairpri in Calathros at Etarlinde" – Etarlinde means between lakes and could describe a location between Loch Etive and Loch Creran in north-east Lorn. Many nobles had fallen in this battle, the annals say, and "Talorgan son of Fergus goes in pursuit of Ainfchellach's son who had taken flight". It is noticeable that the annals specifically refer to Fortriu – if that was, indeed, in northern Pictland, Talorcan would have marched from Inverness through the Great Glen into Dalriada, which after this dual blow was completely in Pictish hands. A conflict with Cenél nGabrain is not mentioned at this point, which can only mean that Kintyre also recognised Pictish rule.

We do not know whether there was unrest in Dalriada, possibly after the death of Cu Bretan in 740, who six years previously had betrayed his brother Talorc to Angus, but in 741 there was yet another Pictish campaign against Dalriada. The main target of Angus' attack seems to have been a man called Indrechtach mac Fiannamail, who traced his descent to the legendary Aidan, who, at the end of the sixth century, had fought successfully against Brude, son of Mailcon. Initially, the *Annals of Ulster* mention a battle near Forboros where two sons of Fiannamail and others had fallen, Indrechtach and Conall. This is confusing, because soon after there is another entry about a second battle, against Indrechtach, in Druimm Cathmail, between the "Cruithin and the Dál Riata" – the Cruithin were the Picts. Neither battle can be located, and there has even been speculation that one of these battles was fought in Ireland where Indrechtach might have fled. This is unlikely. The second entry continues: "The smiting of the Dál Riata by Aengus son of Forgus." This is a significant term, translated from the Latin "percutio" or "percussio". It has been pointed out that the word is used on several occasions in the Latin Bible, the *Vulgata,* usually as acts against individuals. There are also precedents for whole regions, for instance in the *Annales Cambriae,* the *Annals of Wales,* where the "percussio Demeticae regionis" is mentioned, the devastation of Dyfed. We can assume that the use of "percussio" in the context of Dalriada points to a level of destruction that went far beyond the usual, particularly as the Irish chronicles never used this term except on this occasion. This is confirmed by the fact that Dalriada is not mentioned again in the Irish annals for thirty years. Angus seems to have laid waste to Dalriada and probably eliminated large parts of its nobility. It was now a Pictish province.

Before Angus' second engagement in Dalriada, the peace with Northumbria had also broken down. There was no obvious reason for this – or none we know of – and no particular upheaval during the succession on the Northumbrian throne. When war broke out in 740, Eadberht ruled in Northumbria, who was quite an efficient king and profited from the fact that his brother Ecgberht was bishop of York. There has been some speculation that Angus might have hoped to manoeuvre Earnwine into the kingship – his father Eadwulf had possibly been in Pictish exile. Eadberht was in a difficult situation, because almost at the same time he was attacked from the south, by the Mercian king Aethelbald, who was seen as the mightiest king in the British Isles – and he now had an alliance with Angus. Aethelbald crossed the river Trent, in an act of "impious treason" (probably in breach of a treaty) and laid waste to a Northumbrian district. The war at two fronts had no direct consequences for Northumbria, although Eadberht might have been forced to pay tribute to his two neighbours. With the consequence that Pictavia under Angus was now seen as the second-most important power on the British Isles after Mercia – or even on a level with the latter. One chronicle wrote that Aethelbald and Angus had claimed the joint status of British high kings, and the same chronicle notes for the year 750 a West-Saxon uprising against Aethebald and Angus. Whatever the truth behind those stories, there can be no doubt that Pictavia under Angus had reached the pinnacle of its power.

In 744, however, Angus tangled with an opponent that showed surprising limits to his military potency: the Strathclyde Britons. This was the first war between the two; after all, there had been quite close dynastic connections, for instance through Derilei, the mother of two Pictish kings, Brude and Nechtan. There seems to have been a battle, but we know neither its location nor its result – it was obviously not decisive, certainly not a crushing Pictish victory. Strathclyde was ruled by Teudubr, who was distantly related to the Pictish king Brude who had been the victor at Dunnichen. In the preceding decades, Strathclyde had hardly featured at all in the annals, but events in the 740s showed that this tenacious kingdom with its shifting borders could still be a serious player. When the war resumed in 750, the power constellation in northern Britain had changed – Angus was now allied with the Northumbrian king, still Eadberht. And now the Picts suffered a serious setback, the first during the reign of Angus. His brother Talorcan, who we had last encountered in a victorious battle in Lorn, led an army into the territory of Strathclyde (the Britons there were also known as Alt Clut Britons) and was decisively defeated and killed near Mugdock on the northern edge of today's Glasgow. This outcome was obviously seen as highly important, because it was not only mentioned in the Irish annals, but also in the Welsh and Anglo-Saxon chronicle. Some Irish annalists interpreted this as a sign that Angus' power was on the wane, which might also be connected with the rise of Aed Find in Dalriada, who began the task of restoring Scottish sovereignty and who, on his death in 778, was described as "Rex Dail Riata".

Mugdock was hugely important for the Alt Clut Britons – it might well have ensured the continued survival of their kingdom. Teudubr died in the same year, and he was succeeded by his son Dumngall (or Domhnall), who reigned until 760. But what about Angus? There is an enigmatic entry in the *Annals of Ulster* for 750: "End of the reign of Aengus". Had he been toppled, if only temporarily? Irish annals (not Ulster) also mention a battle between the Picts themselves, at Asreth in the district of Chirchind (Circinn), which corresponds roughly to today's county Angus where the battle of Dunnichen had been fought. The sequence of events is important, but we have no information on this: if Talorcan challenged his brother, perhaps defeated him, he would have marched virtually straight away to

81

defeat and his own death at Mugdock. There are also indications of a power struggle with a Brude, son of Mailcon (not to be confused with the late sixth-century king), who also died in 750. Whatever happened to Angus during those months, at the end of the year all his potential rivals had been got rid of, and he ruled unchallenged for another ten years. The Pictish king lists indicate no interruption of his reign, anyway.

Mugdock did not mark the end of the war for the Strathclyde Briton, who might have defeated the Picts but had lost territory to the Northumbrians. Open fighting did not resume until 756, when Picts and Northumbrians undertook a joint operation. The latter marched in a north-westerly direction towards the Clyde, whereas Angus, who must have been at least 70 by this time, crossed the river Forth in Stirlingshire. The *Chronicle of 802* has a precise date when the two armies joined forces – August 1st, 756, at Alt Clut, Clyde Rock, the main fortress of the Strathclyde Britons. And there, we read in the chronicle, the Britons accepted the conditions placed in front of them. No word about a battle. We may assume that the Britons came to the conclusion, despite their victory over the Picts six years previously, that they could not stand up to the combined might of the two strongest powers in northern Britain. We can also assume that the conditions mentioned but not outlined in the chronicle had been negotiated in advance, in Govan, it appears, at the edge of the territory of the Alt Clut Britons. Tribute payments and loss of territory are likely to have been involved. Strathclyde did not disappear, but it was not mentioned again in any chronicle until the ninth and tenth centuries.

There was an aftermath that is somewhat obscure, because it does not really tally with Strathclyde accepting conditions, thus recognising the superiority of the two enemies. The same chronicle reports that the army which had marched to Clyde Rock, had then proceeded to Newanbirig where it was slaughtered almost completely. Newanbirig is mostly identified with Newburgh-on-Tyne near Hexham, although there has been an attempt to place this battle at Newborough near Lichfield, which was in Mercia. It would explain one version of the foundation legend of St. Andrews, which says that Angus son of Fergus had founded the church there as a gesture of thanks to St. Andrew, who had saved him after a defeat in Mercia. This scenario stretches the bounds of credibility – why should three armies have marched – or could have marched – all the way down to the Midlands within three days (!) just to fight a battle which they could have had in the Scottish Lowlands or Northumbria? And that is where it probably took place: Angus and his Pictish army will have marched north, while the Northumbrians were followed by the Britons and defeated in a battle. Whether we can believe the chronicle at all is as much an open question as are the reasons and the circumstances if this chain of events did happen.

After this, we have no more information on bellicose action by Angus, either against the Britons of against Dalriada, which will have been regrouping in the meantime, although there is no reason to assume that the Pictish overlordship was seriously challenged in those years. Under Angus, a unified Pictavia had reached the pinnacle of its power, recognised across the British Isles as one of the strongest entities, possibly the second-strongest after Mercia. In some sense we can say that for the first time, we see an outline of future Scotland, much more so than in the truncated shape of Alba, which succeeded Pictavia after the turbulent years of the Viking invasions. Angus' was a bloody reign, but it seems to have been generally peaceful in Pictavia itself. And prosperous, because this was the period of the great flowering of Pictish art: a large number of the wonderful cross slabs were probably carved during the lengthy reign of Angus, including the stone at Aberlemno with the battle scenes generally connected with Dunnichen. Was it a triumphant monument to a great moment in Pictish history? The artist would have been able to draw on orally transmitted memory of the events that stopped the Northumbrian advance into Pictland once and for all, and the king himself had been born in that very region. Angus is also said to be the largest figure on the famous St. Andrews sarcophagus, depicted as the biblical David, dressed like a Roman emperor, who, as the good shepherd, rends the mouth of the lion.

Angus died in 761, after more than thirty years on the throne. He was certainly over 70 years old, most unusual, especially for a king and even more so for such a warlike king. He did not have a particularly good "press": one English source writes that from beginning to end, he committed bloody crimes, like a tyrannical butcher. But many successful kings of that time can be similarly charged. If the Picts had better recognition for their role in Scottish history, he might well be in the records as Angus the Great.

Angus on the St. Andrews Sarcophagus

DARK AGES

The "Dark Ages": a term often used for the early Middle Ages with their cultural decline compared with Antiquity, with their warring and unstable state entities and with the lack of credible information on what was really happening, and heroic poems like *Beowulf* and *Gododdin* are of very little help, even though, together with sculpture, exquisite jewellery and beautifully illuminated books, they lighten the perceived darkness as far as culture is concerned. But for our purposes, things became just a little darker round about the date of Angus' death. The Venerable Bede had died, his *History* had concluded in 731, and this removed an important source for our period. And it became darker, because new and deadly dangers appeared on the horizon. As far as the Picts are concerned, the task becomes, if anything, even more difficult. Historians have constructed a sequence of events, but this is laden with even more speculation than before, when the narration was often not on a very solid foundation. It now becomes even harder to make a choice between different interpretations of the meagre information.

One factor which has occupied us a great deal so far can now be left to one side: the sources do not mention another confrontation between Picts and Northumbrians, which is not to say that there were no relations, no trade or cultural exchange. There were clearly mutual influences in what has been described as "insular" art, which was quite distinct from what was happening on the continent of Europe. The Picts played a major part in this, with their exquisite sculptures.

There is also the curious story that some Northumbrians were said to tattoo themselves at the end of the century, reported by a papal legate, whereas on the other hand, Pictish tattoos or body decorations are no longer mentioned. And there were still cultural connections between Britain and the rest of Europe (and, no doubt, trade relations): in 781 the Northumbrian king, Aelfwald, sent Alchwini, a monk from York, as an ambassador to the court of Charlemagne. Under the name of Alcuin he became one of the closest advisers of the future emperor and one of the most important philosophers of that time.

But back to Pictavia. Angus was followed on the throne by his brother Brude, son of Fergus, who must have been very elderly and should not be confused with Angus' son Brude, who had been taken hostage in Ireland and died soon after regaining his freedom. Brude died two years later, in 763, and was succeeded by Kenneth (Ciniod), son of Vuredech (or Feradach, who was the brother of Dungal in Dalriada, who had fought against Angus thirty years previously). Dungal had been executed by drowning, while Feradach had stayed at the Pictish court as a hostage and married a Pictish princess, possible a sister of Angus and Brude. Kenneth therefore had Scottish blood in his veins – did he also speak Gaelic? There is speculation that while the Scots had been defeated on the field of battle, their cultural penetration of Pictavia had already begun.

We know very little about weather and climate in northern Britain during that time, but it appears that Kenneth's early reign was overshadowed by a very harsh winter, 763-4. We know about this from Northumbrian sources that mention deep snow right into spring with catastrophic consequences for agriculture. Livestock in the Scottish West where snow is a rarity in the lower-lying regions will have been very badly affected, and we know that in Ireland, there were near-famine conditions even until the end of the 760s. Much snow in winter would lead to flooding in spring and make planting for the following year's harvest correspondingly more difficult. We have no direct information on conditions in Pictland but can assume that they were not so different from northern England and Ireland. The plague in the 660s had spared the Picts – which according to Adomnan was due to the benevolent influence of Columba – but it is unlikely that they were equally lucky on this occasion.

We have no more information about Kenneth's reign than one line in the *Annals of Ulster*, for the year 768: "A battle in Foirtriu between Aed and Cinaed." The traditional interpretation is that this marked the moment when Dalriada cast off the Pictish yoke and invaded Pictland, either in an easterly direction to Perthshire and Atholl or through the Great Glen to Moray. Aed was probably Aed Find of the southern clan Cenél nGábrain, who was, at his death, described as king of Dalriada but was then restricted to the southern regions of Argyll. We know nothing about the outcome of that battle – it was obviously not decisive, as both kings continued unaffected, as it seems.

There is, however, a second interpretation (by James A. Fraser) which sees this battle as an internal Pictish matter. Aed, he thinks, had received his position from the late King Angus, as a kind of governor, and he was in all likelihood related to the future Pictish kings Constantine and Angus, with Fergus, a brother or other relative, being the father of the two kings, who reigned between 789 and 834 and also appear in the Dalriada king-list. Which would mean that in reality, Dalriada was further from independence than ever, had instead been integrated into Pictavia in the form of probably two provinces, with Aed Find being in charge of Atholl and southern Dalriada and Kenneth himself in Fortriu and northern Dalriada. The matter at issue in the battle of 768 would then have been the Pictish crown and not the independence of the Scots. It would throw a completely new light on the later decades of Pictish history, but this hangs on a huge amount of speculation, although it would make more sense than the assumption that the Scots should have been able to challenge the Picts so soon after the devastation visited upon them by Angus.

Kenneth died in 775, and he was followed by Elphin (Alpin), son of Vurad or Vuroid, who, according to the king-list, had only three-and-a-half years on the throne, although the *Annals of Ulster* had him die in 780 and described him, clearly incorrectly, as king of the Saxons – there was no king of that name in Anglo-Saxon history. Perhaps the Picts were holding a slice of Northumbrian territory south of the Firth of Forth. It is probably coincidence that the two kings carried the name of the alleged conqueror of Pictland a few decades later, Kenneth McAlpin. And yet: was there a blood relationship?

There followed a rather confusing period with several kings with contradictory lengths of reign assigned to them by the various sources. It clearly means that Pictland disintegrated into its constituent parts, at least for the time being – it is hard to say, anyway, whether Pictland spent a longer time as a unified kingdom than with more or less independent parts, even if there was a nominal king. This is hardly surprising in view of its geography. Alpin was followed by Drest, son of Talorcan, who is given reigns ranging between one and five years by the various king-lists. A different Talorcan, son of Drestan, appears in only some of the king-lists, and the *Annals of Ulster* add to the confusion by introducing a "Black Talorcan" (Dub Tholargg) into the equation, who was king "on this side of the Mounth" (Rex Pictorium citra Monoth) and who is supposed to have died in 782. From 785, a third Talorcan is mentioned as king, son of Angus (Onuist), who must have been the great warrior king. He, too, spent only three years on the throne, to be succeeded by Conall, son of Tarla (Tagd), king from 788 to 793.

This is all very problematic – the sequence makes little sense, the matrilineal descent does not seem to have been kept, and Conall was probably no Pict. Modern historians have tried to bring it into some kind of order, but only by fiddling with the lists. Tim Clarkson removes Conall completely, as an obvious error, which I cannot accept. Fraser changes the whole sequence without having much to go on, except a more logical development. He starts with "black" Talorcan, identifying him as a son of the great Angus and has him ruling for two-and-a-half years, from 780 to 782, on one side of the Mounth. Drest, son of Talorcan, would have reigned for one year from 780 on the other side of the Mounth, initially jointly with "black" Talorcan. Conall was then king from 785 to 789, possibly alone. If we accept this timeline, Pictavia had split after Alpin's death in 780, and "black" Talorcan had the south as his power base – "this side of the Mounth". Whether Fortriu was in Moray or, as was traditionally assumed, in the south, the latter was clearly becoming the more important part of Pictavia in the second half of the eighth century, and the first version of the *Pictish Chronicle* was probably composed in Abernethy. It also mentions church buildings in the south, such as Abernethy, Dunkeld and Kilrimont (St. Andrews). Whether there had been a civil war among the Picts or whether the kingdom had split peacefully, it is certainly clear that this was a period of considerable instability, and the Picts were lucky that they faced no external challenges during those years.

The uncertainty ended, when the second great Pictish king within a few decades ascended the throne – Constantine (or Causantine), son of Fergus and a grandson of the great Angus. His fame does not rest on mighty deeds, of which we know as good as nothing. But he had a long undisputed reign, until his death in 820, and had a strong reputation well beyond his kingdom's borders, and Pictland remained the most stable entity in northern Britain during the first wave of Viking attacks. His name is first mentioned, however, in connection with a battle, chronicled in 789 by the *Annals of Ulster*: "A battle between the Picts, in which Conall son of Tadc was defeated and escaped; and Constantín was victor." This was obviously the moment when Constantine finally took power, and the uncertainty is reflected by the length of his reign given by different king-lists, which varies between 35 and 45 years. He must have governed some part of Pictavia even before his victory over Conall. If 45 years were to be correct, he would have had a share in the kingdom from the death of Kenneth, which seems rather unlikely as he is not mentioned during the turbulent interval. Connall was not killed in the battle of 789, he presumably escaped into Argyll, his likely homeland, where he finally fell in 807, in a battle fought in Kintyre.

This indicates that the Pictish position in Dalriada had probably been somewhat weakened, after all, but in 811, Constantine also appears in the Scottish king-list, which some saw as a simple error, especially as the chronology of the kings in Dalriada makes little sense in this period. There are two alternatives – one speculates that Constantine and his brother Angus, who succeeded him, were sons of a Fergus, son of Eochaid, who had died in 781 as king of Dalriada. That would have meant that Constantine and Angus were Scots, not Picts, which again seems unlikely. A more realistic scenario would be that Constantine himself took over as king of Dalriada and united the two entities for the first time in what later would be called personal union. He may have installed his son Domnall as a governor or sub-king, because Domnall, son of Constantine, appears in the Scottish king-list, remaining on the throne for allegedly 24 years. The Constantine in question must have been the Pictish king, because another man of this name appears in none of the contemporary sources. It would, incidentally, be an interesting choice of name, possibly inspired by the great Roman emperor.

I have already mentioned that under Constantine, Pictavia remained unaffected by the first Viking raids. They began in 793 when the first known attack hit the Northumbrian coast, plundering and destroying a swathe of coastland, including the monastery on Lindisfarne. That first raid was finally defeated, as we read in a report by Simeon of Durham from the early 12th century, using contemporary sources, when the leader of the

Viking war-band was killed and a storm destroyed the fleet in 794 – which means that this was already more than just a lightning raid, that the Vikings had spent the winter in Britain. For the same year, 794, the *Annals of Ulster* state laconically: "Devastation of all the islands of Britain by heathens." Heathens (or foreigners) was a word generally used for the Norsemen, and Alex Woolf suggests that the chronicle did not insinuate an attack on all the British Isles but probably just the Hebrides (there was a precedence for that usage). This, therefore, would have hit parts of Dalriada. And it continued. In 798, the *Annals of Ulster* say that the heathens had burned Inis Patraic, today's County Dublin, had received tribute in the form of cattle and had penetrated deeply into Ireland and Alba (meaning, in this case, Britain). And in the same year, we hear about the first raid in Wessex, south-west England, a raid probably conducted from Ireland. It appears that the Vikings had first attacked along the east coast, were eventually beaten back there and had then switched to the west coast and very soon started settling down, first in Ireland – tributes of cattle would have made little sense if they had to be carried away in narrow long-ships.

It is, of course, entirely possible, even likely that the first Viking raids started earlier than 793. The Northern Isles (in this case Shetland) are almost equidistant from Norway and mainland Scotland, and the Norsemen, being great seafarers, will have been acquainted with them. Northern mainland Scotland might have seen Vikings much earlier, too, possibly without coming to the notice of the Pictish king, as that area was hardly populated at all, in contrast with the Northern Isles, particularly Orkney. The first Viking war-bands originated from the southern Norwegian mountains, but the larger Viking armies involved in later pitched battles with the Picts and others obviously came from other regions, too, supplemented by other invaders from northern Denmark. There was to be a clear distinction between Vikings and Danes in subsequent developments.

While Pictavia remained substantially unaffected by the early Viking invasions, it suffered damage on the margins. The monastery at Portmahomack was, as mentioned, burned down around this time, between 780 and 830 according to carbon dating. As nothing is known about early Viking raids on Pictavia, we can assume that it happened after 800, possibly even after 820. Generally, however, Pictavia remained a stable factor, which has even led to speculation that Constantine might have done deals with the Vikings, thus deflecting their attacks to other regions or ceding some northern territories. There is no indication of this, but the danger came nearer. For the year 802, the *Annals of Ulster* report that the heathens had burned down Iona, and for 806, that the "community" (translation of Latin "familia") of Iona, numbering 68, had been killed by the heathens. Iona, which was situated right on the shipping lane along the Scottish west coast, was particularly vulnerable, and in connection with this constant danger we have to see the establishment of a new spiritual community, a "civitas", at Kells in Ireland through Abbot Cellach of Iona, not least in order to take Columba's relics to a place of greater safety. Iona was not given up, though, because in 825 a monk named Blathmac was martyred on Iona when he refused to betray the location of Columba's shrine. His death was celebrated by the Rhenish poet Walafrid Strabo, who described Iona as an island off the Pictish coast – possibly confirmation of the theory that Dalriada had to be seen as part of Pictavia during that period. According to a later medieval report, which was added to the king-list, Constantine also founded Dunkeld at that time, which was to be the focal point of the Columba cult in the later kingdom of Alba. Kenneth McAlpin is said to have taken a Columba relic to Dunkeld.

The relative safety of central Pictavia is underlined by the foundation of Forteviot as a royal residence through Constantine. This was particularly remarkable as Forteviot was not fortified, or was at least not situated in an easily-defendable position in the fertile lands south of Perth. It was also proof that the Pictish core territory was, at that point, certainly in southern Pictavia, whether Fortriu was in Moray or not. There is virtually nothing left of Forteviot as it was in the early Middle Ages, but we know there were a wooden residence and various buildings, as aerial photographs have shown, while the Water of May has washed away anything on the surface. There was one impressive remainder, however: on the river bed a sculpted arch was found, the famous Forteviot Arch, now in the National Museum in Edinburgh, and this was certainly part of an early basilica, which must have been stone-built in order to carry the weight of the only true arch found from early medieval Britain. In a piece of impressive detective work, Nick Aitchison interprets the sculpted scenes on the arch as the foundation act of the basilica. While Constantine is generally accepted as the founder of Forteviot, which retained its significance as a royal residence for 400 years, it is first mentioned in connection with his successor, Angus. He was probably the king pictured on the Forteviot Arch, and he is also the king connected with the scarcely believable foundation legends of St. Andrews (a more likely candidate than the older Angus, the great warrior king). And Angus was also in all likelihood the king who commissioned the greatest monument to Constantine – the Dupplin Cross, which stood in a field near Forteviot, until it found its present home in the ancient church at Dunning. It is the only surviving free-standing cross in Pictland and one of the best examples of Pictish art – with the Latin inscription "Custantin filius Fircus", Constantine, son of Fergus. It has no Pictish symbols but Constantine on horseback and as David, the harpist. The king died in 820 and, like that of Angus, his name appears in the *Liber vitae* in Durham, directly after that of Charlemagne.

When Constantine's brother Angus became king, the Irish annals described Constantine and, by implication, his brother as "king of Fortriu", which leads to the conclusion that this was now used to cover the whole of Pictavia, possibly including Dalriada. Apart from Angus' possible role in founding the churches in Forteviot and St. Andrews, we know virtually nothing about him – it means, however, that Pictavia remained an island of stability in the increasingly dangerous environment of Viking attacks and attempts to settle. There are some indications that a certain amount of population movements by Scots into Pictland had begun, which would hardly be surprising as the territories on the west coast were much more at risk from Viking depredation. While this initially had no political influence, a gradual cultural change and shift in the population

Dupplin Cross in Dunning church

structure will have begun (more about this later). Angus died in 834, again described as "king of Fortriu" in the *Annals of Ulster* – as the brother of a long-lived king, he must have reached a considerable age for the time. With him, one of the longest peaceful periods in Pictish history drew to a close.

With his death, the amount of knowledge that has come to us is also further reduced. The Irish annals drew their information on Picts and Scots from Iona. This source had now dried up. The next two kings are not mentioned at all in the Irish sources. The notoriously unreliable *Pictish Chronicle* names two kings that had reigned simultaneously, Drest (Drust), son of Constantine (and thus a nephew of Angus), and Talorcan, son of Vuthoil. They were on the throne(s) for three years, until 836 or 837 – the figures do not add up properly. Whether they were rivals or whether the kingdom had once again split into north and south, is pure guesswork. But the next king, Owen (Uven, Wen, Eoganan), son of Angus, the king who had died in 834, had clearly reunited the country.

The main area of operation of the Viking armies at that point was Ireland, at least if we can rely on the Irish annals – every year, they report lost battles, raids, plunder and destruction. In 839, Pictavia's period of grace came to an end, and when the Viking attack came, it was not an opportunistic raid but an organised campaign, originating from the Viking state around Dublin and probably conducted across the river Clyde deep into Pictish territory. The Picts met this attack with a combined force of Picts and Scots – the location of the battle is unknown but probably in southern Pictland which now clearly was the core territory. It ended with a devastating defeat for the

Picts, and this time, the *Annals of Ulster* knew about it: "The heathens won a battle against the men of Foirtriu, and Eóganán son of Aengus, Bran son of Óengus, Aed son of Boanta, and others almost innumerable fell there." Bran was Owen's brother, Aed was the king of Dalriada, probably a sub-king installed by the Picts, who will have left the Scots little choice whether they wanted to fight by their side. In retrospect, it was one of the most important battles in early medieval Scottish history, because it launched a period of change that was to lead to the "disappearance" of the Picts.

At first, the Vikings seem to have disappeared fairly quickly, undoubtedly laden with booty and slaves. In Pictland, a period of great confusion followed. One king-list has two short-lived monarchs, Vurad (Wrad, Ferat, Feradhach), son of Bargoit, with three years on the throne, and then a king named Bred, for just one year, whose ancestry is unknown. A different list gives three further kings: Kenneth, son of Vurad, for one year, Brude, son of Vuthoil, two years, and Drust, son of Vurad, three years. These figures do not tally with the alleged takeover by Kenneth McAlpin in 843; they must represent a series of complicated power struggles which Kenneth (Cinaed, Ciniod) eventually won. He had reportedly taken power two years earlier in Dalriada, very soon after the lost battle against the Vikings.

And this is where it ends according to the traditional interpretation, which some historians still accept, for instance Tim Clarkson in his 2008 history of the Picts. It is a tempting story that makes superficial sense. There were clearly power struggles in a badly weakened Pictavia that had disintegrated into several entities, and Kenneth, having quickly restored a well-organised Dalriada, was easily capable of defeating each of the other pretenders – thus the traditional story-line. The historical myths seem to confirm this story – one example being the *Cronica Regum Scottorum* from the 12th century, in which Kenneth leads his Scots with wondrous cunning from Argyll into Pictland ("Hic mira calidate duxit Scotos de Ergadia in terram Pictorum"), where he bloodily eliminated the weakened Pictish ruling class and replaced them with Gaelic-speaking Scots, who saw to it that the Pictish language and culture disappeared without trace. The most famous myth was the so-called "Treachery of Scone" (or rather Forteviot), related in 1214 by Giraldus Cambrensis in his *De Instructione Principum*. This story has the Scots invite the Picts to a banquet, at which they were generously plied with food and drink, and when they were sufficiently bamboozled, the Scots "noted their opportunity and drew out the bolts which held up the boards; and the Picts fell into the hollows of the benches on which they were sitting, in a strange trap up to the knees so that they could never get up; and the Scots immediately slaughtered them all …". Another version saw them fall on blades erected below the platform. It is interesting that Gerald of Wales' sympathies are entirely with the Picts, who had invited the Scots, their allies, into their country and who, as the far superior people in terms of numbers and bravery, could only be defeated by this act of treachery, which he says was inbred and typical for that nation. The Picts, on the other hand, had expected no such thing, as the Scots had been tied to them by good deeds and comradeship. With this, the more warlike and mightier nation had disappeared altogether.

There were various similar stories, which obviously had a common origin. The *Huntingdon Chronicle* from the 12th century wrote:

> And in the seventh year of his reign – when Danish pirates had occupied the shores, and with the greatest slaughter had destroyed the Picts who defended their land – Cinaid [Kenneth] passed over into, and turned his arms against, the remaining territories of the Picts; and after slaying many, drove the rest into flight. And so he was the first of the Scots to obtain the monarchy of the whole of Alba, which is now called Scotia; and he first reigned in it over the Scots. In the seventh year of his reign he fought seven times in one day with the Picts, destroyed many, and confirmed the kingdom to himself, and he reigned for twenty-eight years.

When Huntingdon talked about Danes, he meant Vikings, because by the 12th century, the difference between Vikings and Danes, who invaded later, had faded. And fighting seven times in one day with the Picts has to be seen symbolically – apart from being an impossibility, the use of the number seven points to this very clearly. The lingering sympathy with the Picts – or a lingering Pictish tradition well into the Middle Ages – is also reflected in a very similar but somewhat confused tale in *The Chronicle of the Picts and Scots* that refers to the death of the allegedly last Pictish king, Drust, at Forteviot:

> As the chronicles testify, a son of a king of Ireland, called Redda, arrived in Galloway, and, partly by prow-

ess and by affinity of Irish blood, with whom the Picts were mixed, occupied that country, and also Argyll and others of the isles, the issue of whom, who called themselves Scoty, always plotted against the Picts until in the time of this Drust, son of Feradhach, the Scots contrived a conspiracy, and at a general council were privately armed, and in the council-house slew the aforesaid king and all the great lords of the Picts, who did not think of evil. They sent afterwards for such others as they wished, and slew them as they came, so that they did as they desired; and from that time henceforth the kingdom of the Picts failed, which had lasted for eleven hundred and eighty-seven years, and the kingdom of the Scots recommenced, which had commenced before the Picts, four hundred and forty-three years before the incarnation. The Picts destroyed in this manner, Kynet son of Alpin reigned over the Scots, and was the first king of the Scots after the Picts.

Kenneth McAlpin as the victor in a bloody power struggle, with the stories about the treacherous massacre symbolising the destruction of the Pictish ruling class, and Kenneth as the founder of a dynasty which turned Pictland into Alba, this is, as I have already mentioned, the traditional view of the events after around 840. There would have been attempted Pictish uprisings, but they were all defeated by a determined and powerful monarch ("seven in one day"). But things were not quite as clear-cut as that.

END OF THE PICTS?

Modern research is split on what really happened after the disastrous defeat against the Vikings and the rise to power of Kenneth McAlpin. To start off with, it has always been known, from the Irish chronicles, that Kenneth died as "king of the Picts", and so did his immediate successors. While Tim Clarkson, for instance, sticks to the story of a violent takeover by the Scots, another modern author, W.A. Cummins, claims that virtually nothing changed at all. The Scots had already disappeared from the sources, and the last king of Dalriada identified as such had died in 792 (Donncorci). What remained throughout the ninth century, were kings of Fortrenn and then of the Picts, and only when the Irish annalists (Cummins writes) changed from Latin to Gaelic, Pictavia was replaced by Alba. Apart from that, nothing had changed: "the same dynasty, the same kingdom, the same people". The same goes for English and Welsh sources during the ninth century, who called what Cummins describes as the "Picto-Scottish people" Picts, the words Alba or (Latin) Albania were not mentioned. And when the Picts disappeared in the *Anglo-Saxon Chronicle* before the end of the ninth century, there was no Alba, there were Scots and Scotland. Here, too, according to Cummins, the disappearance of Pictavia was a function of the switch from Latin to the vernacular. But something did change – the Pictish language disappeared, and at this point, I cannot agree with Cummins who says that it was pushed back by the forward-march of English. Of course this happened, but it was Gaelic that clearly became prevalent in large parts of Scotland, the names of places, mountains, rivers etc. are silent witnesses. Whether this happened at the rapid pace that is usually suggested remains, in my view, an open question. We shall come back to this matter.

This period, like most others in Scottish early medieval history, suffers from the poverty of the sources. In the *Annals of Ulster*, for instance, we learn nothing about Kenneth, except for his death. We have to fall back on later medieval chroniclers, who were reproducing second- and third-hand material that was losing authenticity on every step. There are two principal "sources" – one is the *Chronica Gentis Scottorum* by John of Fordun, written towards the end of the 14th century, i.e. more than 500 years after Kenneth's rise to power. The other one lies in the Bibliothèque National in Paris and has been known since 1729, containing seven documents on 296 folio pages – among them a Pictish chronicle in extracts from Isidor of Seville, the so-called A version of the Pictish king-list, a *Cronica Regum Scottorum*, a version of the foundation legend of St. Andrews and a chronicle of the kings of Pictavia and Albania, ranging from 843 to 995, which had been written or compiled around 1360, commissioned by Robert of Poppleton, who became prior of a Carmelite monastery in Northumberland in 1364. It obviously relies on earlier authors, like Gerald of Wales, and has to be treated with the usual caution. This problematic document might be the best we have, but it contains no dates, just the lengths of the various reigns. However, the dates can be verified through other sources. The chronicle might have been written during the reign of the last king on the list, Kenneth (II.), son of Malcolm (Cinadius filius Maelcolaim), who ruled between 971 and 995, but the length of his reign was left open in the list – the author might not have known. A further complicating factor lies in the fact that the events given for the various kings' reigns are not contemporary but were added later, which even the language shows at times. For instance, the use of the word "Danari" (Danes) for the reign of the first Kenneth is clearly anachronistic, as this word, in the Gaelic form "Danair" only appeared after 980 in the Irish chronicles.

But let us start with what the *Chronicle of the Kings of Alba*, as it has become known, says about Kenneth McAlpin. I follow the translation given by Alex Woolf with minor corrections from the original Latin.

> Kinadius then, the son of Alpin, first of the Scots, ruled this Pictavia happily [traditionally translated as "successfully", but the original Latin says "feliciter"] for xvi years. Pictavia, moreover, was named from the Picts, whom, as we have said [a misleading reference], Cinadius destroyed. For God condescended as reward for their wickedness, to make them alien from, and dead to, their heritage; they who not only spurned the Lord's mass and precept but also did not wish to be equal to others in the law of justice. He, indeed, two years before he came to Pictavia, assumed the kingship of Dál Riata. In the seventh year of his reign he transported the relics of Saint Columba to the church he had built, and he invaded, six times, Saxony and burned Dunbar and occupied Melrose. Also the Britons burned Dunblane and the Danes laid waste to Pictavia, to Clunie and Dunkeld. He died eventually from a tumour before

the ides of February, on a Tuesday, in the palace of Forteviot.

We have, as I said, no idea when this text was written – but certainly not earlier than a century and a half later, because only then were the Danes mentioned. Seen in the connection with the previous Pictish king-list, this looks just like a continuation, especially as both are usually printed together. Dalriada is mentioned, almost as background information, as it appears, and we can assume that this is correct. But in which function? Was he really a Scot, or was Kenneth a Pict? The name Alpin appears in Dalriada but not in Ireland – Woolf speculates that it might have been a British name. Or was Alpin a version of the Pictish Elphin – Ciniod son of Elphin? Between 763 and 780 the brothers Ciniod and Elphin ruled in Pictland. If Kenneth was indeed a Pict, then his ascension to the throne would have been no more controversial than one of the usual internal power struggles, and he might have ruled in Dalriada as a kind of Pictish sub-king. We can assume that at a time when intermarriage must have been very common, the real situation will have been somewhat more complicated. Cummins states that to the Scots, Kenneth will have been a Scot, and to the Picts, a Pict. But as his "obituary" states: he ruled as king of the Picts.

Another factor against the traditional idea of a bloody subjection of the Picts is the statement that he ruled "feliciter", happily. He also seems to have had the strength to conduct an expansive foreign policy, to which a struggle with latent Pictish resistance would have been hardly conducive. He obviously was able to exploit the weakened state of Northumbria that was to disappear completely for a time under the pressure of Vikings and Danes (and Picts, it seems), because while Melrose is today in the Scottish border country, it was then well into Northumbrian territory. Under the given circumstances we can assume, on the other hand, that Scots were settling in large numbers in Pictavia, because Dalriada was simply no longer safe. This was also behind the story that Kenneth was taking Columba's relics to Dunkeld (obviously shared with Kells), to a church that Constantine might have started already. Dunkeld had been mentioned for the first time in 865. But, as the chronicle shows, it was not immune from Viking attacks. Columba's relics will also have been accompanied by the returning Columban clerics, a majority of whom, of course, spoke Gaelic. There were no doctrinal problems any more – Iona had long accepted the Roman versions of Easter and the tonsure, but it should be mentioned that the beginning transition from Pictish to Gaelic cannot have been easy for the population. While the two branches of Celtic were probably closer to each other than they are now, we should not forget Adomnan's story that Columba and King Brude needed an interpreter at the end of the sixth century. Kenneth's kingdom was also attacked by the Britons – the first sign of activity from Strathclyde, since their alleged defeat of the Northumbrians after they and the Picts had dictated a peace around a hundred years previously. No date is given, but we can assume that they tried to exploit Pictish weakness after the heavy defeat against the Vikings.

Meanwhile, the situation surrounding the Vikings also became more complicated, with the appearance of the first Danes, described as "black heathens (or strangers)" by the Irish annalists, not yet as Danes, in contrast to the "white heathens" from Norway. They were no allies – after a Danish fleet attacked the Viking settlement near Dublin, there was a two-year war between the two, which the Norwegians won, forcing the Danes and the local population to pay tribute. While the Vikings eventually settled on the Northern Isles and in northern Scotland, the Danes became the main factor in England, but this is outside the scope of this small book. It appears that Argyll itself (excluding the islands, which had been lost) was at that point largely free of Viking attacks, perhaps related to the story that Kenneth's alleged father Alpin had married a Scandinavian princess, with whom he had a son named Domhall, who would have been Kenneth's half-brother. Kenneth was in alliance with a Northern Irish king of Scandinavian extraction, named Guthfrith mac Fergus, whose territory reached across the water into Lorn. But he fell in the fighting between Vikings and Danes. All this was, in the end, no protection against another Viking raid (Danes in the chronicle) that brought destruction as far as Clunie and Dunkeld. It was probably just another plundering expedition, no attempted conquest, and no battle is mentioned, but it demonstrated the continuing vulnerability of the Pictish state, despite the fact that it seems to have recovered much of its old strength under Kenneth – who died peacefully, if possibly painfully, in Forteviot.

While Kenneth had strengthened his realm, it was much smaller than Pictavia had been at the height of its power, before the Viking invasions. The Northern Isles and the north mainland were both lost, and we know virtually nothing of events in Moray, which is now mostly accepted as Fortriu.

108

Portmahomack had already been destroyed, the monastery replaced by secular workshops. It appears that Dingwall marked the southern boundary of Viking expansion, but there are many fantastic stories about the fighting there. I have, for obvious reasons, grave doubts about the theory of a controlled invasion by the Scots of the Cenél Loairn clan in Argyll into Moray, while their countrymen form Cenél nGabráin are supposed to have taken over the Pictish south. Is it really possible to trace a sequence of place names for an event that is supposed to have been accomplished within decades? One thing is clear: the balance of power lay now clearly in the south, and the extent of connections between north and south is entirely unknown in this era.

Kenneth was succeeded in 858 by his brother Domnall – Donald in modernised form. The name could be British or Gaelic, and he must have been fairly old when he ascended the throne; he lasted only four years, and in 862 the *Annals of Ulster* reported the death of Domnall, king of the Picts. The king-list has a correspondingly short report, with an interesting twist:

> Dunevaldus (Duuenaldus), his brother, held the kingdom iiii years. In his time the rights and laws [iura ac leges] of the kingdom, of Áid son of Eochaid, were made by the Gaels [Goedeli] with their king at Forteviot. He died in the palace at Cinnbelathoir [Cinn Belachoir] on the ides of April.

The king mentioned here was Aed Find, son of Eochaid, who had died in 778 and who seemed to have gained a certain degree of autonomy for Dalriada after the destruction by Angus. The usual interpretation of this passage assumes that Donald created a legal basis for the conquest of the Picts through the Scots by forcing Gaelic law upon the Picts. This was not necessarily the case – two kings seemed to have been involved in this particular meeting ("cum rege suo"), which could mean that Donald concluded a compact with the king of Dalriada, who would have been some kind of sub-king in the fragile condition of the west. This would be thinkable in either scenario, whether, in this case, Donald was a Pictish or a Scottish king. Alex Woolf speculates that they might have sworn an oath cementing good relations. But the passage certainly does not exclude the unification of legal systems – and we should never forget the dubious nature of the source material we are dealing with. The place name mentioned, Cinnbelathoir, was probably near today's Scone, soon to become the centre of Alba.

The succession then went to Kenneth's son Constantine, who reigned from 862 to 877 and died, like his predecessors, as king of the Picts. This is what the chronicle had to say about him.

> Constantinus son of Cinaed reigned xvi years. In his first year Maelsechnaill king of the Irish died and Áed son of Niall held the kingdom, and after two years Amlaíb, with his heathens, laid waste to all Pictavia and occupied it from the first of January to the Feast of Saint Patrick. In the third year, yet, Amlaíb, drawing tribute [the Latin word here is "centum", a hundred, but no other translation makes sense], was killed by Constantin. After a short while, in his fourteenth year, a battle was fought at Dolair between the Danair and the Scotti

110

and the Scotti are slain at Achcochlam. The Normanni [Norsemen] spent a whole year in Pictavia.

According to the *Annals of Ulster*, Constantine (again "rex Pictorum") died in 876, which makes his reign 14, not 16 years, but that could be a mistake by the scribe, because the Roman numerals were easy to confuse. The name is interesting – while some historians tried to see him as a descendant of the earlier Constantine, it could have been chosen as a conscious reminder of the great king. The Viking attack on the Picts is confirmed by the Irish annals, where it says for 866: "Amlaíb and Auisle went to Fortriu with the Gaill [heathens] of Ireland and Britain, plundered the entire Pictish nation and took hostages from them." Only the chronology is a little out – this was not the third year of Constantine's reign, but we can assume that the Irish annals were dating more reliably than the account in the king-list, which was written at a much later date.

Amlaib (or Olaf in modern terminology) was an important Scandinavian leader, who was first mentioned by the *Annals of Ulster* in 853, in a raid on Ireland which had much more the character of a conquest than a mere raid. Auisle (or Asl) was said to be his brother, whom he had killed in 867. These men – from Laithland, the location of which is unknown – had been in Ireland since 840, fought subsequently against the Danes, before they ganged up with them; Olaf and the Danish leader Ivarr arc mentioned repeatedly in joint action. Whatever the dating, the invaders stayed for some time in Pictland – Woolf assumes in Fortriu, the northern districts, but I find this unlikely, as the centre had clearly shifted to the south. Furthermore, the interchangeable terminology Fortriu/Pictavia seems to indicate that what was really meant was the south, whatever the original location of Fortriu had been. We simply know far too little about the north where we would have expected Viking raids coming from further north.

It can certainly not be correct that Constantine killed Olaf in his third year (but the third year could conceivably refer to a different starting date, especially if the chronicle has gaps). Olaf was heavily engaged in military action after the withdrawal from Pictavia, accompanied by hostages to guarantee good behaviour. For the year 869 we read in the *Annals of Ulster* of plundering and burning in Armagh, mass killings and abductions and raids by Olaf. And in 870 Vikings and Danes, led by Olaf and Ivarr, attacked the Strathclyde Britons and laid siege to Dumbarton. It was a bitter fight, and Dumbarton finally fell after four months, after which it was destroyed so thoroughly that it was not mentioned again in any source until the 13th century. And in 871 Olaf and Ivarr returned with two hundred ships from Britain to Dublin, with many Angles, Britons and Picts as prisoners, according to the *Annals of Ulster*. It must have been a wide-ranging expedition. Artgal, the king of the Strathclyde Britons, was killed in 872 – on the instigation or advice ("consilium") of King Constantine. We are not told, what the king's actual role or motivation was, but by then, he might have defeated the Vikings and killed Olaf – when Ivarr died in 873, he was described as king of all Norsemen in Ireland and Britain. During the raid that included the destruction of Dumbarton, the Norsemen might have imposed tributes on some more Pictish districts, and Constantine reacted with a successful battle. He might then have tried to use this for gains against the weakened Strathclyde Britons and got rid of their king in the process, now with cooperation by the Scandinavians.

But Constantine was unable to retain the upper hand. The last year of his reign brought another decisive defeat, this time against a Danish army – that the chronicle identified the invaders correctly as Danes can be seen from the *Annals of Ulster*, which registered for 875: "The Picts encounter the Dubgaill [Black Heathens] and a great slaughter of the Picts resulted." The fact that the chronicle speaks of "Scotti" should be seen against the terminology of the Irish annals, which was contemporary. It seems that the Danes mentioned in the annals had landed in East Anglia in 865 and by the end of the following year, had conquered large parts of Northumbria, up to the river Tyne. This became known as the "Great Army" in English historiography, also known as "Scaldingi", which could mean that they were part of the Danish contingent which had occupied Belgium during large parts of the ninth century (referring to the Schelde river, or Scheldt). The *Anglo-Saxon Chronicle* reports for 875: "Healfdene went with part of the army into Northumbria and set up winter quarters by the river Tyne, and the army conquered the land and they often ravaged among the Picts and the Strathclyde Britons." This Healfdene was, incidentally, driven out of Northumbria by his own army – because of his extreme body odour, if we can believe the *History of St. Cuthbert*, but the Danes settled down in Northumbria so quickly that by around 900, stability had temporarily returned, in the shape of an Anglo-Danish kingdom.

The losing battle that marked the beginning of the end of Constantine's reign was fought at Dolair, which was almost certainly Dollar in Clackmanshire, in the extreme south of Pictavia. It would have been easy for a Danish fleet to sail up the Firth of Forth. The Scandinavians spent a whole year there, according to the chronicle, provisioning and plundering, and won a second battle at "Achcochlan" which is generally assumed to refer to Atholl. That is where Constantine died, according to a later chronicle at a place called Inverdubroda or Inverdufat, which might refer to a tributary of the river Tay. The *Annals of Ulster* date his death to 876, the chronicle has 877.

Constantine was followed by his brother Áed, who had a short and unhappy reign, from either 876 or 877 to 878. There might have been a short intermission, which would point to rather chaotic conditions coinciding with occupation through the Danes. The note in the chronicle is equally brief:

> Edus (Aed) held the same for one year. The shortness of his reign has bequeathed nothing memorable to history. He was slain in the civitas of Nrurim.

And the *Annals of Ulster*: "Áed son of Cinaed, king of the Picts, was killed by his own companions." The Latin word is "socii", which might refer to members of his own household. Nrurim has not been identified positively, but a king-list from the 12th century tells us that he was killed in battle in Strathallan by Giric son of Dungal – and Strathallan contains only one "civitas" (major church settlement), and that is Dunblane. There might have been an older name which is now lost. There is another note in the Irish chronicle referring to 878 that points to the collapse of security in Pictland: "The shrine of Columba and his other relics arrived in Ireland, having been taken in flight to escape the Gaill."

We have now reached the moment when the name "Picts" disappeared from the chronicles. Aed was the last king whom the Irish chronicles described as "Rex Pictorum", and the Anglo-Saxon chronicles mentioned the Picts for the last time in connection with the campaign conducted by the Dane, Healfdene. It seems to coincide with a particularly confusing period, although this could be a function of the extreme poverty of the sources. Until 900 we have nothing but the now rather garbled history reflected in the Poppleton manuscript. This is what it says about the successor(s) of Aed:

> Eochodius [Eochaid], then, son of Rhun king of the Britons [Strathclyde], grandson of Cinaed [Kenneth] by a daughter, reigned xi years; but Ciricius [Giric] son of ? reigned then because he became the *alumnus* and *ordinator* of Eochaid. In his second year Áed son of Niall died and in his ix year on the very day of *Ciricius* there was an eclipse of the sun. Eochaid with his *alumnus* was expelled then from the kingdom.

There are two dates in this text, which was obviously written much later – the death of the Irish king Aed, who indeed died in 879, and the eclipse of the sun, which was on June 16th, 885, which was the feast day of one of several saints called Cyriacus. But the text gives the year 887, which therefore was clearly wrong, and the scribe had been confused, because he first wrote xi, then crossed the "i" out and placed it before the "x", thus changing eleven into nine, which got him somewhat nearer to what must have been the correct date. If both Eochaid and Giric had been expelled immediately after the eclipse, the length of the reign given for Eochaid was wrong.

If Eochaid reigned at all. The son of a king of Strathclyde and a grandson of Kenneth, who thus became part of the Alpinid line, was not mentioned anywhere else, just in the Poppleton manuscript. The formula that he did not really reign but had Giric as a kind of teacher and "prime minister" to guide him is quite unique in the chronicle, and this very Giric is given as king by other authors – much later ones. A thirteenth-century addition to some versions of the Scottish king-list says that Giric "conquered all of Ireland and the greater part of England [Anglia], and that he first gave liberty to the Scottish Church, which, up to that time, had laboured under the customs and mores of the Picts". The so-called *Dunkeld Litany* was even later in the form in which it has come down to us – it was a liturgical text rescued from Dunkeld at the time of the Reformation and taken to Regensburg in Germany. Woolf thinks that this text had an ancient core, and it contains a prayer imploring God to "protect and defend our king Girich and his army from all the intents of his enemies and concede to him victory and long life". In the 12th century, he was even described as "Gregor the Great", in connection with his liberation of the Scottish church from the Picts. It is a mystery that offers no easy solution. It would be hard to believe that one of the two, most likely Eochaid, was simply invented – the kingdom might have split, and Eochaid might have been a sub-king under Giric, who was to develop the bigger reputation. But we know nothing about his family background, because Poppleton

116

simply says: "Licet Ciricium filium alii dicunt his regnasse" – whose son? Perhaps even Eochaid's son? But we do not know Eochaid's age, who might have played an important role as carrier of the Alpinid dynasty and was needed to have been recorded as a king for the historical tradition to continue.

In 900, the change of name became, as it were, official, when the *Annals of Ulster* and chronicle of the Scots announced that "Donald (Domnall), son of Constantine, king of Alba died". There is a slight divergence here, because another translation of the *Annals of Ulster* says "king of the Scots" – but certainly no longer "king of the Picts". The much later Poppleton chronicle still uses mixed language in its brief relation of Donald's reign:

> Donald (Donivaldus) son Constantine held the kingdom xi years. The Norsemen laid waste to Pictavia at that time. In his reign occurred a battle at Innisibsolian between the Danes (Danarios) and the Scots (Scottos): the Scots had the victory. At Dunnotar he was slain by the heathens.

The Latin original of the last sentence is "Oppidum fother occisum est a gentibus", and that has been translated generally as "Dunnotar was destroyed by the foreigners/heathens". Grammatically, this is tempting, but "occidere" simply does not mean "to destroy", it means "kill, slay". Nothing is dated in this notice to break down the eleven-year reign of Donald (889-900), but it was obviously turbulent, with major destruction by the Vikings, a victory against the same enemy (more likely Vikings invading from Ireland than Danes) and a violent death. The location of the battle is undetermined, but the name seems to

117

indicate one or several islands, which in all likelihood would have been on the Scottish west coast in Argyll. After the interval with Aed, Eochaid and Giric, the throne had now returned to the Alpinids, as Constantine had been Kenneth's son. We can assume that Donald had been a minor at the time of his father's death.

We have, indeed, now reached the end of the Picts, at least in the sense of their name. An Irish source, a version of the *Lebor Bretnach*, a Gaelic reworking of the *Historia Brittonum*, confirms this, if that is not too strong a word: there had been seventy Pictish kings, from the legendary Cathluan until Constantine, who had been the last, and that was Constantine, son of Kenneth. But why Alba, which obviously was more than just a linguistic switch from Latin to Gaelic, especially as Alba also had a Latin version, Albania? Alba was originally the Gaelic name for the whole of Britain (as in the modern Albion) – comparable to the use of "America" for the U.S.A.? It would be interesting to know how the Picts described themselves, in their own language, when they did not use the Latin term. Later Welsh sources used the word "Prydyn" when describing Scotland, but, of course, this is the same word as Britain – and for themselves, they finally settled on Cymru. Cruithne, the Irish name for the Picts, was the Q-version of the British "Prydyn", as Dauvit Broun explains. He also points out that Albid may have been a Pictish word – corresponding to the Welsh "Elfydd", meaning world, earth, land, districts or neighbourhood. That could mean that Alba was actually derived from the Pictish language and may have been in use for much longer,

118

then adopted by the Alpinids as a compromise for the mixed Gaelic-Pictish nation. But this is, of course, speculation.

It would make sense to end the story of the Picts here. But a better form of "closure" is provided by one of the most important kings of the period, yet another Constantine, who was not only remarkable for his long reign, from 900 to 943. He then retreated into a monastery where he died in 952. He must have been very old. His reign marked an important turning point in Scottish history, because it included a first contact between recognisably English and Scottish kings, thus prefiguring much of later Scottish history. He has the longest entry in the Poppleton chronicle. Constantine II, as he became known, was the son of Aed, who had followed his brother, Constantine I, on the throne for just one year, and this meant that he was also the grandson of Kenneth McAlpin. Three years after he had gained the throne, he was faced with another Viking invasion hitting, according to Poppleton, Dunkeld and "the whole of Alba". But a year later, Constantine managed to turn the tables on the Vikings, defeating them in "Strath Erenn", a battle in which "the men of Fortriu" (*Annals of Ulster*) killed the Viking leader Ivarr, grandson of Ivarr, and caused great slaughter. This is the last time that Fortriu is mentioned in the chronicles and was the basis for situating it in the southern half of Pictland, not least because of the connection with Strathearn. Woolf, who relocated Fortriu to Moray, points out that the river Findhorn was also originally called Earn. But it seems highly unlikely that the battle was fought in Moray, but could the "men of Fortriu" have marched south? We had already seen that "Fortriu" had become something of a generic term for the whole of Pictland/Alba. This might well apply here, too. Wherever it was – this battle marked a turning point in the Scandinavian wars, because from then on, Scotland remained safe from Scandinavian raids from the south. The north was a different matter.

In 905/6, Scone was mentioned for the first time – on the Hill of Belief ("collis credulitatis" – the translation as "belief" is slightly questionable), Constantine and Bishop Cellach had come together to pledge "the laws and disciplines of the faith and the right of the Church and the Gospels equally with the Scots" ("pariter cum Scottis"). The "Hill of Belief" is probably a low mound still visible today, and this act has usually been interpreted as conclusion of the takeover of the Pictish church by the Gaelic church of Iona. According to Woolf, it might have been no more than a ceremony – but the fact that the Irish church was becoming paramount in the former kingdom of the Picts is undeniable.

The next major event in Constantine's reign was a battle against the Danish king Raegnald (Gaelic Ragnall, in Old Norse Rögnvaldr), fought well outside Alba, down by the river Tyne in Northumbria. The *Annals of Ulster* have an unusually detailed report:

> The foreigners [heathens] of Loch dá Chaech, i.e. Ragnall, king of the dark foreigners, and the two jarls, Oitir and Gragabai, forsook Ireland and proceeded afterwards against the men of Scotland. The men of Scotland, moreover, moved against them and they met on the bank of the Tyne in northern Saxonland. The heathens formed themselves into four battalions: a battal-

120

ion with Gothfrith grandson of Ímar, a battalion with the two jarls, and a battalion with the young lords. There was also a battalion in ambush with Ragnall, which the men of Scotland did not see. The Scotsmen routed the three battalions which they saw, and made a very great slaughter of the heathens, including Oitir and Gragabai. Ragnall, however, then attacked in the rear of the Scotsmen, and made a slaughter of them, although none of their kings or earls was cut off. Nightfall caused the battle to be broken off.

Poppleton also mentions this battle, with the Scots winning, while a different chronicle has Constantine following an appeal for help by the Northumbrian prince Ealdred and losing the battle against Raegnald. It was obviously an important event with a fairly open outcome which allowed both sides to claim victory. It certainly did no harm to Constantine's position.

Meanwhile, there had been far-reaching changes in England. The process of integrating the Scandinavians had started, and in the early tenth century, the Saxon king Athelstan, the grandson of Alfred the Great, more or less managed to unite the whole country. As part of this, he seems to have received the Northumbrian crown in 927 and, according to one chronicle, accepted the subjection of all British kings, among them the Scottish king, Constantine. And he was able to substantiate this position. In 934, Athelstan took an army to Scotland, accompanied by three Welsh kings, 18 bishops and 13 dukes, six of whom had Danish names. Simultaneously, a fleet sailed to Scotland. The *Historia Regum Anglorum* (History of the English Kings) tells us that he suppressed his enemies, laid waste to Scotland up to Dunnotar and the "mountains of For-triu" and raided Caithness with his fleet – Caithness was of course part of the Viking state that came to be based on Ork-ney. The report on this in the *Anglo-Saxon Chronicle* marks the first occurrence of the term Scotland. The reason for this major invasion, if we can believe the chronicles, is obscure – it might have been connected with Ealdred's death in Northumbria and a possible attempt by Constantine to meddle in the succession, which Athelstan would have seen as his prerogative.

The fact that Athelstan was the supreme British leader was underlined by events when he was back in southern Eng-land in September 934, in Buckingham, where Constantine seems to have been in his train, because a gift authorised by Athelstan was witnessed, among others, by "Constantin *subregulus* [sub-king]". Constantine was still there in 935, be-cause at a grand court in Cirencester no less than five kings were present, led by Constantine, who must have been around 60 by then. Owain of Strathclyde was next in the order of rank. But Constantine must have feared for his position in Alba, be-cause by Christmas Owain was "number two" after Athelstan, Constantine was obviously back in Scotland.

Athelstan had reached the height of his power – he in-tervened in Franconia, where his nephew Louis gained the throne, in Brittany where an English fleet participated in the change of ruler and possibly even in Norway. But there were dangers at home, arising in Ireland where the new Scandinavian king, Olaf (Amlaib), had gained the undisputed power and turned to England to pursue his claim to the Northumbrian throne. This brought him into collision with Athelstan, and in

937 they clashed in the famous battle of Brunanburh in which Constantine fought on Olaf's side against the Anglo-Saxon army. The location of Brunanburh has never been settled, but speculation concentrates on a place near Liverpool, today's Bromborough. This is how the *Annals of Ulster* saw it:

> A great, lamentable and horrible battle was cruelly fought between the Saxons and the Norsemen, in which several thousands of Norsemen, who are un-counted, fell, but their king, Amlaíb, escaped with a few followers. A large number of Saxons fell on the other side, but Athelstan, king of the Saxons, enjoyed a great victory.

No doubt, Athelstan saved the unity of England, but not for long: he died two years later, and his kingdom unravelled quickly – Olaf fulfilled his wish despite his defeat and became Northumbrian king, but Constantine's position was now secure, and so was that of the emerging Scotland.

Events in the northern lands of Pictavia, in Moray/Fortriu, during this period are almost completely obscure. We do not even know who reigned there, assuming that the kings in the chronicles were restricted to the southern region. It appears that the institution of the above-mentioned "Mormair" developed during this period, as predecessors to regional earls or even sub-kings, who organised the country and warfare with the Vikings. Otherwise, there is a theory that for a time from the tenth century kings alternated between south and north, between the descendants of the two sons of Kenneth McAlpin, Aed and Constantine. This is by no means certain. In the eleventh century, Macbeth of Shakespeare fame or infamy was said to be the first king to re-unite the two parts of rump Scotland, the old northern and southern regions of Pictavia. Meanwhile, there are blood-curdling stories of wars between the inhabitants of Moray and the northern Vikings in the Norse sagas, which prove only that those were uncertain times with fluctuating fortunes. Although we only hear of Scandinavian victories, the fact remains that Dingwall marked the southern boundary of the Scandinavian sphere of influence which was to become the dukedom of Orkney. We know from the archaeological evidence that the monastery at Portmahomack was burned down and that the Tarbat peninsula was a strategically important point to hold, for harbour and shipping lanes, but what happened to the bishopric of Rosemarkie is entirely unknown, until much later in the Middle Ages.

This atmosphere of mystery also surrounds one of the grandest Pictish monuments of them all, "Sueno's Stone" in Forres. With a height of six metres, it is certainly the biggest carved stone slab on the British Isles. One side is completely covered with battle scenes – but which battle? The stone was discovered in the 18th century and probably had a neighbour. It appears to stand near where it was originally placed. Carbon dating of the wooden pedestal on which it stands indicates a date in the tenth century – post-Pictish therefore, but in character it is entirely Pictish. The name Sueno's Stone refers to the Danish king Sven Tveskaeg ("Forkbeard"), who died in 1014 in England, but this was in all likelihood a mistake. But which battle or war was it? It could have been a successful fight against the Scandinavians, or perhaps a campaign by Alba against the men of Moray, as the *Chronicle of the Kings of Alba* (Poppleton)

124

reports for Malcolm I (943-954) ("With his army Malcolm proceeded to Moray and slew Cellach."). We know nothing about Cellach. Fordun's later chronicle, written in the Middle Ages, says that Dub MacMalcolm (962-66) had been killed by the men of Moray near Forres, but Fordun is notoriously unreliable. All we can say is that Sueno's Stone is witness to the fact that the Picts might have disappeared by name but that their culture was very much alive when it was sculpted.

We know the end result: Scotland became largely Gaelic, for a time, at least, until English took over. It is hard to believe that this process was concluded in a matter of decades. Informed opinion now largely discounts the traditional story of a violent takeover by the Scots under Kenneth McAlpin. He might have been a Pict himself (or half-Pict), and in the balance of power, the Picts had had very much the upper hand for a century or so. But they had suffered a crushing defeat at the hands of the Vikings in 839. It will have left their ruling class heavily depleted. Picts and Scots fought together then, but I suspect that the Scots were under the command of the Picts and that the latter suffered bigger losses by the very nature of early medieval warfare. Some Scots will have used the opportunity to slip into vacant positions, take over as office holders or landowners where the previous occupants had been killed. This would have been facilitated by the small numbers involved – we are talking about a ruling class of a few thousand at most, possibly fewer. I think that it belongs into the realm of historical fiction, when an eleventh-century source, from the time of Malcolm, son of Kenneth, who reigned from 1005 to 1034, "assigns" the various areas to Gaelic clans from Dalriada: the

Sueno's Stone, Forres

area between the rivers Forth and Tay to Cenél Comgaill, the areas further northeast towards Aberdeen to Cenél nGabrain and Cenél Oengusa, today's Aberdeenshire to Cenél Conaing and Moray to Cenél Loairn. The latter clan was said to have migrated through the Great Glen, leaving a track of Gaelic place-names in its wake. This "arrangement" bears all the hall-marks of later rationalisation.

Of course, there can be little doubt that the majority of the Dalriadan population settled in the former Pictland. By the time of the Viking invasion, this process seems to have been well underway, as I hinted earlier. It was not the case, as Cummins postulated, that nothing happened at all, that only the name changed but that the people remained the same and that Pictish as a language had been swept away by English moving north through Scotland. Gaelic won out, even though its retreat began as early as the 12th century. But how long did Pictish survive among the people? Did it really disappear that quickly? Did most of the Picts speak Gaelic as early as 930, as Dauvit Broun speculates? There is certainly evidence of early Gaelic penetration of Pictland – the name "Atholl" for instance means New Ireland, and in Fetteresso parish in The Mearns, we find the so-called "Lang Stone of Auquhollie" with an Ogham inscription of a kind otherwise only found in Ireland. But I think that the main settlement movement did not start until the ninth century when Pictavia was, for a time, much safer from Viking raids than the exposed land on the west coast. Pictish kings might have actively supported this population movement, with, in the long run, fatal consequences for their own culture.

127

This, after all, seems to be the crucial factor in my view. The Vikings were the joker in the pack. They triggered the Scottish "invasion" of Pictavia. And with the Scots, the Columban church returned, having been expelled by King Nechtan in the early eighth century. While church business and church services were all conducted in Latin, the majority of Columban clerics will have had Gaelic as their first language. Now it was back, and in the changing political situation, they might have seen less need to adapt to their parishes where, in any case, there was probably more Gaelic spoken than two centuries before. The church was the greatest cultural influence, and this will have been one of the prime movers for the progress of Gaelic among the Picts. There was no longer anything remotely as powerful in Pictish culture and politics. In addition, Gaelic existed in writing, whereas we have no evidence that anything was ever written down in Pictish. The Picts did write, Portmahomack proves this, but it will have been in Latin. There was a cultural imbalance which, in my view, was probably decisive. On the other hand, there is some evidence that the Pictish land settlement survived; the various "Pit" names (usually a combination of the Pictish "Pett" and a Gaelic name) indicate this.

While academics argue over the fate of conquered peoples – did they mix with the new rulers, or were they, in some cases, exterminated? – this does not apply in the case of the Picts and the Scots. There were, in my reckoning, roughly four times as many Picts as there were Scots. Even if the Picts accepted culture and language, they did not go away. And they are still here. Genetically, the population of Scotland, with the exception of the Lowlands, will be more Pictish than Scottish. This is, of course, totally irrelevant. But it is of some interest to wonder what would have happened if the Vikings had not appeared on the scene. Scottish history would have taken a very similar route, and in language terms, Scotland would be as English as it is today. But early medieval history, as it was composed in subsequent centuries, would have had different traditions, would have been written with different interests in mind. And the geography would sound very different, mountains, rivers and villages and towns. Anyone for Aberness?

NOTES ON THE LITERATURE

Many of the sources can be found on the Internet, the Pictish king lists for instance and the *Annals of Ulster*. Adoman's *Life of Columba* is a Penguin Classic, and I have used the Oxford World Classics edition of Bede's *Ecclesiastical History of the English People*. Modern historical studies of the Picts began with William Forbes Skene (1809-1892) and his three-volume work *Celtic Scotland: A History of Ancient Alba*, Edinburgh 1876-80. He also edited a selection of sources under the title *Chronicles of the Picts, Chronicles of the Scots*, Edinburgh 1867, which can be downloaded from Google Books. Much of that is in Latin. Modern academic research began with F.T. Wainright (ed.), *The Problem of the Picts*, Edinburgh 1955, with essays based on the first Scottish archaeological "Summer School", 1952 in Dundee. The classic study, which is still valuable today, is Isabel Henderson, *The Picts*, New York 1967. There are still many valuable insights, particularly on the interpretation of Pictish symbols, in Elizabeth Sutherland, *In Search of the Picts*, London 1994, which was my first introduction to the subject. Anyone interested in the Picts should read this book. Other general studies are Lloyd & Jenny Laing, *The Picts and the Scots*, Stroud, Gloucestershire (Sutton) 1993; Sally M. Foster, *Picts, Gaels and Scots*, London (Historic Scotland) 1996; W.A. Cummins, *The Age of the Picts*, Stroud (Sutton) 1995; Stephen Driscoll, *Alba. The Gaelic Kingdom of Scotland AD 800-1124*, Edinburgh (Historic Scotland) 2002. The first attempt to write a coherent history of the Picts was made by Tim Clarkson, *The Picts. A History*, Stroud (Tempus) 2008. Stuart McHardy, *A New History of the*

Picts, Edinburgh 2010 adds nothing to the debate and should be treated with the utmost caution. Some of his views and interpretations are very strange, and he is largely unaware of the latest research. The most important new works, on which I have relied heavily, are the first two volumes of the new *Edinburgh History of Scotland* by the two leading authorities in this field; James E. Fraser, *From Caledonia to Pictland. Scotland to 795*, Edinburgh 2009, and Alex Woolf, *From Pictland to Alba 789-1070*, Edinburgh 2007.

There is a lot of literature on the symbol stones, which I have not covered in this short book. I merely wish to mention W.A. Cummins, *The Picts and their Symbols*, Stroud (Sutton) 1999, and the magisterial and richly illustrated book by George and Isabel Henderson, *The Art of the Picts. Sculpture and Metalwork in Early Medieval Scotland*, London 2004. This book is indispensable. There are many studies on special subjects, which I shall not mention in detail here; I would only like to draw the reader's attention to the series of lectures, published in article form, by the Groam House Museum in Rosemarkie. There are some important special studies in book length, which I have made use of: Nick Aitchison, *The Picts and the Scots at War*, Stroud (Sutton) 2003; Nick Aitchison, *Forteviot. A Pictish and Scottish Royal Centre*, Stroud (Tempus) 2006; James Fraser, *The Pictish Conquest. The Battle of Dunnichen 685 and the Birth of Scotland*, Stroud (Tempus) 2006; Martin Carver, *Portmahomack. Monastery of the Picts*, Edinburgh 2008; Leslie Alcock, *Kings and Warriors, Craftsmen and Priests in Northern Britain AD 550-850*, Edinburgh (Society of Antiquaries of Scotland) 2003.

131

This book is a shortened version of my own illustrated book on the Picts in German, *Die schottischen Pikten. Geschichte und Mythos eines rätselhaften Volkes*, Greiz (König) 2012. This includes chapters on Pictish art and excursions on various subjects based on the above-mentioned special studies.